Nations Without Nationalism

European Perspectives

**Other works by Julia Kristeva
published by Columbia**

*Desire in Language: A Semiotic Approach
to Literature and Art*

Revolution in Poetic Language

Powers of Horror: An Essay on Abjection

The Kristeva Reader

Tales of Love

In the Beginning Was Love: Psychoanalysis and Faith

Language: The Unknown

Black Sun: Depression and Melancholia

Strangers to Ourselves

The Samurai

Nations Without Nationalism

Translated by Leon S. Roudiez

Julia Kristeva

Columbia University Press
New York

Columbia University Press
New York   Chichester, West Suxxex

Columbia University Press wishes to express its
appreciation of assistance given by the government of
France through La Ministère de la Culture in the
preparation of this translation.

Copyright © 1993 Columbia University Press
All Rights Reserved

French edition, *Lettre ouverte à Harlem Désir*
© 1990 Editions Rivages
English translation, Translator's Introduction, and "What of
Tomorrow's Nation?"
© 1993 Columbia University Press

Library of Congress Cataloging-in-Publication Data

Kristeva, Julia, 1941–
    [Lettre ouverte à Harlem Désir. English]
    Nations without nationalism / Julia Kristeva ; translated by Leon
S. Roudiez.
      p.   cm.
    Includes index.
    ISBN 0–231–08104–9
    1.National characteristics, French.   2. Racism—France.
3. Nationalism—France.   4. Désir, Harlem, 1959—Philosophy.
5. Gaulle, Charles de, 1890–1970—Philosophy.   I. Title.
DC34.K7513   1993
305.8'00944—dc20   92–23568
                                                                CIP

                                   ∞

                   Casebound editions of
              Columbia University Press books
                           are printed
                 on permanent and durable
                        acid-free paper.

               Book design by Teresa Bonner
         Printed in the United States of America
               10 9 8 7 6 5 4 3 2 1

EUROPEAN PERSPECTIVES
A Series in Social Philosophy and Cultural Criticism

Lawrence D. Kritzman and
Richard Wolin, Editors

European Perspectives seeks to make available works of
interdisciplinary interest by leading European thinkers. By
presenting classic texts and outstanding contemporary
works, the series hopes to shape the major intellectual
controveries of our day and thereby to facilitate the tasks of
historical understanding.

Julia Kristeva	*Strangers to Ourselves*
Gilles Deleuze	*Empiricism and Subjectivity*
Theodor W. Adorno	*Notes to Literature,* vols. I and II
Richard Wolin	*The Heidegger Controversy: A Critical Reader*
Antonio Gramsci	*Prison Notebooks,* vol. I
Pierre Vidal-Naquet	*Assassins of Memory*
Alain Finkielkraut	*Remembering in Vain: The Klaus Barbie Trial and Crimes Against Humanity*
Jacques Le Goff	*History and Memory*

CONTENTS

Translator's Introduction

Three of the essays translated here
were published together, in the
original French, as *Lettre ouverte à
Harlem Désir* (Paris: Rivages, 1990).
The title essay and the interview
dealing with *The Samurai* origi-
nally appeared in Philippe Sollers's
L'Infini (No. 30, Summer 1990),
while "The Nation and the Word"
came out in an undated [June 1990]
special issue of *Le Nouvel Observa-
teur* on the occasion of what would
have been De Gaulle's one hun-
dredth birthday. The liminary essay, "What of Tomorrow's Nation," was written specifically for
this translation; since Julia Kristeva had a different public in mind,
one that would not have read her
more theoretical texts, she does,

in part, go over some of the ground covered in *Strangers to Ourselves* (Columbia University Press, 1991).

The notion of "strangeness" is what holds these essays together. It is one that has been with her for the past quarter of a century, from the time when she came to Paris from her native Bulgaria. Even there, I suspect that a feeling of difference, if not strangeness, was already weighing on her consciousness. Her upbringing and education were somewhat unusual, as French nuns started molding her mind before Communist youth organizations took their turn. Her father, Stoian Kristev, was an intellectual, an eminent scholar who was never integrated into the party cadres (he died in 1989). When Julia Kristeva came to Paris she held a doctoral fellowship in French literature; the topic she investigated for her *doctorat d'université* was the emergence of a different genre (or text, as she preferred to call it) out of the interweaving of other preexisting genres (or strands of texts). With hindsight, I can see a similarity with the way new nations are born, out of the commingling of individuals and groups of individuals with different cultural, religious, and political backgrounds. Thus Gauls, Romans, Visigoths, Franks, Basques, Normans, and others eventually merged into the nation we call France; Anglo-Saxons, Dutchmen, Hispanics, Irish, Germans, Africans, Scots, Swedes, Russians, Chinese, Japanese, and other Asians are still struggling to constitute an American "nation"—while the American Indians, once on the verge of extinction, are now winning some recognition.

When Kristeva's interests soon shifted in the direction of linguistics and semiology and she wrote her monumental *La Révolution du langage poétique* (1974, partly translated as *Revolution in Poetic Language*, Columbia University Press, 1984), which one might term a study of the "strangeness" of French poetic language in the nineteenth century, she became interested in the child's entry into language—how this utter stranger became (or failed to become) assimilated into the surrounding linguistic domain. The step into psychoanalysis now seems inevitable; integrated as the child might appear to be, it remains active in the shadow of an adult's consciousness and is indeed the stranger within. One might think of a string of dichotomies—stranger/neighbor, fearsome/familiar, irrational/rational, and semiotic/symbolic—in which the first term is often the more significant in determining human behavior.

In those works that I view as making up a trilogy, *Powers of Horror*, *Tales of Love*, and *Black Sun*, Kristeva has examined the basic components of the human psyche from historical, religious, sociological, psychoanalytic, and literary points of view. While the words *strange*, *strangeness*, or *stranger* seldom if ever appear in those essays, the notion of "otherness" is ever present. Since then, the notions of "strange" and "other" have merged, and in *Strangers to Our-*

selves the final emphasis is on the stranger within, the other within the same.

Concurrently Kristeva has come to see De Gaulle as the giant stranger who could not accept the prevailing mediocrity of his time; this would account for his historical successes as well as for his failures. Her novel, *The Samurai,* in addition to being an attempt to account for the intellectual life in Paris since the late sixties, is a story involving strangers; a few are foreigners but all are strangers in the sense that they are intellectuals who live apart from most other human beings. Like the aristocratic samurai of feudal Japan they have their own rituals and often fight among themselves, although their victories are not so bloody. Many ordinary people would like to have them disposed of, but Kristeva argues that all otherness needs to be understood and accepted.

The same would be true of all ethnic, religious, social, and political differences. Some commonality must be found and Kristeva sees this key in Montesquieu's notion of *esprit général,* which is explained and discussed in the first essay. This might be a first step in the direction of a nation of strangers and a universe of nations without nationalism. In other words, a better world for tomorrow.

Nations Without Nationalism

What of Tomorrow's Nation?

Why Bother with Origins?

Recently, everyone has been harking back to his or her origins—you have noticed it, I suppose? Some proudly claim their French, Russian, Celtic, Slovene, Moslem, Catholic, Jewish, or American roots—and why shouldn't they? Others are sent back to and blamed for their Jewish, Moslem, Catholic, Kurdish, Baltic, Russian, Serb, Slovak, or American background— and why not? It may happen that the former turn into the latter and vice versa according to the political situation and the ups and downs of the identity struggle that human beings have been waging forever, one that has henceforth lost its ideological masks and is being carried out protected only by the shield of origins. The values crisis and the fragmentation of individuals have reached the point where we no longer know what we are and take shelter, to preserve a token of personality, under the most massive, regressive common denominators: national origins and the faith of our forebears. "I don't know who I am or even if I am, but I belong with my national and religious roots, therefore I follow *them*.[1] Thus does the contemporary Hamlet soliloquize, and it is a rare person who does not invoke a primal shelter to compensate for personal disarray.

What after all amounts to withdrawing into a family seems understandable when one is confronted with the bankruptcy of Marxism and the wounds the latter has uncovered: particularly the humiliation that progressive doctrines have wreaked on national and religious realities. It portends, however, along with ethnic, national, and religious conflicts, a decline of individualities, cultures, and history. In years to come it is likely that we could witness a loss of concern for personal freedom, which was one of the essential assets in the *Declaration of the Rights of Man and Citizen*, to the advantage of subjective, sexual, nationalist, and religious protectionism that will freeze evolutionary potentialities of men and women, reducing them to the identification needs of their originary groups.

The cult of origins is a hate reaction. *Hatred of those others* who do not share my origins and who affront me personally, economically, and culturally: I then move back among "my own," I stick to an archaic, primitive "common denominator," the one of my frailest childhood, my closest relatives, hoping they will be more trustworthy than "foreigners," in spite of the petty conflicts those family members so often, alas, had in store for me but that now I would rather forget. *Hatred of oneself,* for when exposed to violence, individuals despair of their own qualities, undervalue their achievements and yearnings, run down their own freedoms whose preservation leaves so much to chance; and so they withdraw into a sullen, warm private world, unnameable and biological, the impregnable "aloofness" of a weird primal paradise—family, ethnicity, nation, race.

A defensive hatred, the cult of origins easily backslides to a persecuting hatred. And wounded souls may be seen to turn around and fight their neighbors who are just as hurt as they are—perhaps by the same totalitarian tyrant (political or religious)—but who can easily be taken for the weak link in that chain of hatred, for the scapegoat of one's depression.

As an expression of hatred the glorification of origins hence finds its matching opposite in the hatred of origins. Those who repress their roots, who don't want to know where they come from, who detest their own, fuel the same hatred of self, but they think they can settle matters by fleeing. On the contrary, devotees of origins anxiously seek shelter among their own, hoping to suppress the conflicts they have with them by projecting them on others—the strangers.

The recourse to psychoanalysis entails, among other benefits, the production of one of the rare discourses that avoid such symmetry; it invites us to come back constantly to our origins (biographies, childhood memories, family) in order better to transcend them. "This is why a man must leave father and mother" (Genesis 2:24; Matthew 19:5; Mark 10:7; Ephesians 5:31). What if Freud alone allowed us to come close to carrying out that biblical and evangelical exhortation?

The Christian religion, which dominates our West, and the secular thought that has effected its decisive reversal have long been efficient laboratories where such identification hatred could be metabolized, without, for that matter, voiding the commission of crimes. Nevertheless, today's values crisis, beyond the refinements in religious and ideological systems, affects the core of the speaking being; the latter is actually made up of a splitting, a clash between our symbolic identity having strong brotherly demands and our imaginary identity rooted in the original cell (family, race, biology). The problem that develops on account of national and religious conflicts, immigration and racism, henceforth touches upon the fragile boundary that defines civilization and humankind. Before fantasizing about an apocalypse or a new salving religion, let us try to confront a few aspects of the national issue as European, and particularly French, society experience it, without forgetting the echoes that their history and current manifestations might give rise to in American or English readers who come from a different national tradition.

We must recognize that, traditionally and schematically, France is not a privileged focus of attention—either for American political thought or for the so-called average American. Too materialistic or too Catholic, too centralized or too individualistic, too haughty or too archaic, too stylish or too anarchistic, too cosmopolitan or not enough so, too oppositional and not enough "of the people," France fascinates but is not an example to follow. Caught as it is today between an important immigration flow within its frontiers (coming notably from the Maghreb but also from black Africa, Asia, and central Europe) and strong competition from its European partners, France is undergoing a crisis in national identity. The outbursts from the far right represented and exploited by the National Front, as well as the rebuttals issued by young immigrants and antiracist organizations, among which "SOS Racism,"[2] are a good indication that we have reached a crux in the thinking about national French identity and also its reality.

Beyond the opening of borders and the economic and even political integrations that are taking place within Europe and throughout the world, the nation is and shall long remain a persistent although modifiable entity. Will France be able to welcome without too many clashes the flow from the other side of the Mediterranean? Will it be able to play its part as a competitive, cultural, and also economic power in the new European framework and with respect to the pressure on the part of countries of the former Communist bloc who wish to be integrated as soon as possible into a European confederation—a hypothetical one at the moment? Will France finally, taking into account its historical, cultural, and political bonds with the Mediterranean countries, serve as a bridgehead for the establishment of what has been called a Mediterranean serpent that needs to attain secularism and peace in order to insure the beneficial development of individuals within those masses whose numbers are on the increase in North Africa, an area where local resources do not seem able to sustain their expansion?

Here are some of the topics that will appear like watermarks within the text of the brief essays collected in this book. For in the present context, a reflection involving an audience wider than that of academic circles seems necessary where the concept of nation is concerned—a concept that has welded the coherence of individuals in Western history since the eighteenth century. Whatever its antecedents might have been, the idea of the nation was finally molded by the French Revolution.[3] Nevertheless, in the very bosom of the West, this idea includes variations (French nation, German nation, American nation [or union], British nation [or Commonwealth], and so forth) that need to be recalled briefly, important as it is not to reject the idea of the nation in a gesture of willful universalism but to modulate its less repressive aspects, keeping one's sights on the twenty-first century, which will be a transitional period between the nation and international or polynational confederations.

"Contractual" or "Organic": What Kind of Nation Is There in America Today?

Many things distinguish the histories and the concepts of the American and the French nations. France evolved into a unified whole over a span of centuries during which it became lastingly solidified. By the time it thus became a nation, the original thirteen states had barely formed their union, one that was nearly destroyed less than a hundred years later.

In spite of the coming together of the many pieces that have made up the "French mosaic," an administrative sturdiness—comprising economics, culture, and language—turned this country into a base where foreigners can put out roots only if they accept its identity. Foreign transplants are of course fruitful and not as rare as one tends to believe.[4] Nevertheless, for the past twenty years or so, the assimilation drive of the new migrants emphasizes above all the desire to enjoy social benefits and does not at all involve giving up their own typical, behavioral, religious, cultural, or even linguistic features. What sort of common life and what degree of mixing remain possible under such conditions?

America, a country of immigrants, of whom many became westbound migrants, did not *at the beginning* experience the difficulty caused by newcomers confronting a nation that was welded together and dominant. Each one of the early divisions, New England, the Middle Atlantic colonies, and the South had a certain unity but none was truly homogenous. "Contractual" nation or "organic" nation? The German-American political philosopher Francis Lieber discussed the matter after 1856 in what was then Columbia College and vaunted the virtues of the American nation for having resolved the relationships between sovereignty and liberty, between local government and central government, between the republic and the family of nations. Nonetheless, neither the American ethnic polyvalence nor the advantages of a federalism that links independent states resulted in a polyphony resistant to racism and xenophobia. More or less isolationist according to the ups and downs of the economy, a form of an American nationalism hardened during the nineteenth century.[5] Everyone knows, however, that this American nationalism has established hierarchies within itself: New England over the South, the East over the West, and, in dramatic fashion, after the western territories were gradually admitted or annexed into the Union and the problem of slavery exploded in the shape of the Civil War, it bred the difficulty of absorbing into the "American dream" a large number of blacks—who are joined today, often antagonistically, by Hispanic and Asian immigrants. Reality seems to remain distant from the generous wishes that the laws of the Union nevertheless aspire to fulfill and as they were still expressed at the beginning of this century.[6]

To be sure, the American ethnic polymorphism and federalism ("an undestructible nation of undestructible states") have held out better than anything against Nazi barbarity and Communist totalitarianism. The twentieth-century United States excelled in welcoming the victims of the two great plagues of modern times, encouraging and guiding the struggles against them and at the present time favoring the growth of the newest and most challenging currents of thought and art germinating on the Continent. Nevertheless, beginning in 1921, through and after the Second World War, the admittance of refugees to the territory of the United States came up against a quota system based on national origins; a global policy for refugees was not set up until the Refugee Act was adopted in 1980. In the meantime, the national origins quota system of immigration had been abolished in 1965 and later a set of preferential or conditional procedures was introduced (parole programs).

After the enactment of the Refugee Act, geograph-
ical and ideological restrictions defining refugees were
abandoned and American law is in tune with the
Geneva Convention in this respect, without for that
matter forgetting to favor those refugees who are "of
special humanitarian concern to the United States."
Various political motivations, however, may well be
included in that rather fuzzy definition and lead to
sleights of hand or, for instance, in a protectionist
intent, to the creation of a "special entrant" status on
the fringes of the law and without that immigrant
enjoying all social benefits. This instance of legal
confusion merely demonstrates how difficult it is to
follow the law more than it betrays an intent to sway
public opinion, which considers itself outwardly faith-
ful to the traditional view of America as a land of
immigrants but asserts itself as being more and more
turned in on itself and practices protectionism when
confronting the demographic, political, and economic currents (Cuba, Vietnam, Latin America) that
the international situation produces. Restricting the
number of immigrants, integrating those who have
been accepted within American values while allowing
a margin for the assertion of ethnic, linguistic, and
cultural identities—the problems of immigration in
the United States, in all their specificity, are not
dissimilar to the problems posed by immigration in
France.

Thus, in a very different fashion but perhaps still

more painfully than in European states, the United States suffers in its immigrations, which, from within, challenge not only the idea of a national "organism" but also the very notion of confederacy (particularly through the establishment of new immigrant islands whose autistic withdrawal into their originary values is not easy to deal with). Furthermore, the cohesion of the American nation centered in the Dollar and God keeps troubling those for whom the future of men and women is centered in other values. The fierce struggle for profits, a war as *holy* in Washington as it is in Baghdad but in the name of another god and with incomparable humanitarian precautions (since the *Rights of Man* imposes certain duties): are those truly "national values" the entire world, other "nations," "ethnicities," and "origins" must submit to?

What Is a British National?

As to the notion of foreigner according to British common law, this is a difficult matter to elucidate; for on the one hand anyone born on crown territory is a British subject but on the other each country in the Commonwealth may forbid or restrict access to its territory to inhabitants of other members of the Commonwealth.[7] The quality of British subject, bestowed by the British Nationality Act of 1945 and complicated by the dominions gaining independence, means that a person's nationality (his or her citizenship) with respect to international law does not imply that such a person is a foreigner in another country of the Commonwealth, particularly in the United Kingdom. But several recent laws, such as the Commonwealth Immigrants Act of 1962, a second law in 1968, and a third in 1971 that distinguishes between "partial" and "nonpartial" citizens, make the situation somewhat muddled: there are British subjects who cannot freely have access to parts of the Commonwealth and especially to the United Kingdom. The British Nationality Act of 1981 simply refrains, under those circumstances, from defining a British national.

Such caution protects the subjects' presumed equality while leaving the door open for various restrictions and prohibitions. Without going any further into a commentary on the economic and racial probabilities underlying such policies, one might raise another question. Does not the manifest tolerance of the ethnicities and religions that are included in the notion of British subject, which does not invite them to share an *esprit général* but claims to respect their particularities, end up in *immobilizing* the latter and perpetuating the racial or religious wars that are shaking up the Commonwealth as well as the United Kingdom? Of course, the matter of opening up the U.K. to what is outside remains entire: even the European integration continues to upset British political circles, not to mention the social, political, and cultural access to the United Kingdom on the part of individuals

even more "foreign," and thus outside the Commonwealth, who run up against an ancestral rejection
comparable to the one witnessed in France and elsewhere.

These brief references to a few British and American difficulties concerning matters of national identity and immigration will perhaps convince readers
that the considerations I am setting forth here, starting from the experience of European culture up to the
Enlightenment and Freud and from the current French
situation as that country confronts foreigners, are not
without relevance where their own present affairs are
concerned.

The Nation, Yes! But SOS! Racism!

Revising many mental precipitations coming out of
Marxism or abstract cosmopolitanism thus leads us to
question the vitality as well as the therapeutic, economic, political, and cultural value of the *nation*.
Since readers will, in succinct fashion, find such a
reappraisal in the following pages, I should, at the
outset, like to point out that it is being conducted in
the shape of a dialogue with those who, with strength
and determination, are fighting against the degener-
acy of the national idea—that is the association known
as *SOS Racisme*.[8] Founded by Harlem Désir, it is a
group of young people comprising immigrants and
children of immigrants but also many "old-stock

Frenchmen" who reject the xenophobia, racism, and antisemitism of the National Front; they have chosen as their slogan "Don't bug my buddy" ("Ne touche pas à mon pote"), and as their emblem a raised hand— open, held out. Through parades for equality of rights, concerts, and demonstrations, SOS Racisme compelled recognition as a generous, political, and "re-laxed" group; early on it had 350 local committees and 50,000 sympathizers. And a magnificent concert on June 15, 1985, attended by hundreds of thousands in the Place de la Concorde, succeeded in engraving in the minds of all Frenchmen SOS Racisme's image and message. Aside from seeking media attention they are fighting for voter registration of those known as beurs (a phonetic approximation of "Arab" said back-wards, the children of people born in the Maghreb) as well as for giving immigrants the right to vote. Harlem Désir was born in 1959 to an Alsatian mother and a father from the [French] West Indies and has a master's degree in philosophy; his seemingly predes-tined name is not at all a pseudonym, and he steers, along with his "buddies," a group with which finan-cial backers and intellectuals soon became associated. There is a problem: is a joyful appearance enough to offset the danger presented by Jean-Marie Le Pen? Let us go further, let us think: France, that means us, are we agreed? Or do you disagree?

With its ups and downs, the group has made its way while other similar or competing associations take up and diversify its actions and its objectives. *SOS Racisme* is more than a movement: through it and in Harlem Désir's person, the book you are holding speaks to the anxiety of our compatriots, bringing together political and cultural items published in France as various events occurred.

What Position Do I Speak From?

Whence do you speak? This is what distrustful people always ask, and they are not wrong in doing so. It is rightful that I introduce myself.

The one writing here is a representative of what is today a rare species, perhaps even on the verge of extinction in a time of renewed nationalism: I am a cosmompolitan. Admittedly, the term has covered excessive positions, some denying national determinations; these I do not share and shall attempt to examine them critically. Furthermore, I am willing to grant the legitimacy of the ironic objection you might raise: it is beneficial to be a cosmopolitan when one comes from a small country such as Bulgaria, as it is apparently more advantageous to be in favor of the European Community if one comes from Holland rather than from the quiet, powerful traditions of Britain. Nevertheless, I maintain that in the contemporary world, shaken up by national fundamentalism on the one hand and the intensive demands of immigration on the other, the fact of belonging to a set is a matter of choice. Beyond the *origins* that have assigned to us biological identity papers and a linguistic, religious, social, political, historical place, the freedom of contemporary individuals may be gauged according to their ability to *choose* their membership, while the democratic capability of a nation and social group is revealed by the right it affords individuals to exercise that choice. Thus when I say that I have chosen cosmopolitanism, this means that I have, against origins and starting from them, chosen a transnational or international position situated at the crossing of boundaries. Why does such a choice make its way through France and a certain conception of nationality elaborated by the French Enlightenment? Why does intellectual work postulate or at least favor such a fate? Why is the situation of a woman in Europe today congruent with that choice? Those questions will remain just beneath the surface of my remarks and I shall try to give them, if not exhaustive answers, at least the start of meditations for you to pursue.

The difficulty inherent in thinking and living with *foreigners,* which I analyzed in my book *Strangers to Ourselves,*[9] runs through the history of our civilization and it is from a historical standpoint that I take it up in my work, hoping that confronting the different solutions offered by our predecessors would make our present-day debates on immigration more lucid, more tolerant, and perhaps more effective. From that history of the reception Europe had in store for foreigners beginning with ancient Greece, I shall select five moments that seem to me particularly informative as an introduction to the present essays.

Barbarians, Metics, or Citizens of the World

The first foreigners mentioned in Greek mythology are women—the Danaides, whose adventures Aeschylus pieced together in *The Suppliants* (493–490 B.C.). Io, the priestess of Hera in Argos, was beloved by Zeus and thus aroused the jealousy of Hera, his legitimate wife, who avenged herself by changing Io into a frenzied heifer, doomed to be exiled. Io then ceaselessly wandered before settling in Egypt where she gave birth to the kings of Egypt, among whom were Aegyptus and Danaus whose children were the fifty Egyptiades and the fifty Danaides. Descendants of this prestigious ancestor, the Danaides were foreigners for a double reason. First, they were born outside of Greece, did not speak the language, and had strange customs; and then, those women, unamenable to Greekness, were refractory to marriage. The Danaides refused to marry their cousins who, to be sure, were not very attractive, and the women ended up murdering them on their wedding night— according to the most dramatic variation on the myth. What can be seen in this narrative is the distorted memory of the transition from endogamous society (marriage takes place between blood relations) to exogamous society (one selects a spouse from a "foreign country"—outside the family, the clan, the lineage). The Danaides acknowledged the violence that underlay the marriage bond: a pact between strangers, marriage was based upon repressed or quelled aggression, which is so preconscious in the Greek texts that the Danaides, far from being satisfied with everlastingly pouring water into their famous sieve, replaced the symbolic *water* of domestic life with the *blood* poured during the initiatory ceremonies relating to the worship of Demeter and her sacred Thesmophoria.

Let us now leave open the trail on which political strangeness and estrangement between the sexes intersect (I shall return to it briefly toward the end of my present survey) and come back to Aeschylus. Having come to Greece, the foreigners/Danaides can be welcomed on condition that they become "suppliants": before the temple of Zeus the suppliant (protector of foreigners) they must lay wreaths and accept their father's advice of restraint: "Let no boldness / Come from respectful eye and modest features. / Not talkative nor a laggard be in speech: / Either would offend them. Remember to yield: / You are an exile, a needy stranger, / And rashness never suits the weaker."[10]

The Greeks, from whom we have inherited the words *barbarous* (based on onomatopeia: bla-bla—the incomprehensible language uttered by those who do not share the Greeks' mother tongue) and *metic* (resident foreigner, *homo economicus,* the status of one who agreed to contribute to Greek economy but lived in the suburbs and had no succession rights) have elaborated subtle considerations on immigration, in which they balance a concern for benefiting from foreigners with one to keep those foreigners removed from Greek citizenship. I shall not here go further into the details of those considerations and the institutions they spawned aside from mentioning *proxeny* and *prostasia.* The *proxenus* (a word that, like the French *proxénète* [that is, a pimp], came to refer specifically to the protector of those women who engage in a trade as strange as it is archaic, and in that sense a fundamental if not a natural one) and *proxeny* in Greece were at first individual and spontaneous functions and eventually ended up being a public one. The proxenus protected and represented foreigners in the city-state and was appointed, on the basis of his civic merits, by a decree of the polis, whose interest he looked after. *Proxeny* and *prostasia* were not a means of integrating foreigners but existed in order to promote exchanges among foreigners, and they express a political pragmatism that doubtless applies better to citizens of other Greek city-states (there was no question of integrating non-Greeks within the civic structure; the Egyptian Danaides constitute a rare, privileged instance since they, too, benefited from *proxeny*); they also testify to the beginnings of *civic protection* for the foreigner in ancient Greece.

Median wars, Peloponnesian wars, increasing business and travels multiplied the contacts between Greeks
and non-Greeks; that contact, at the same time as it
contributed to forming the notion of Athenian civic
coherence (*koinonia*) according to Aristotle's *Politics,*
also favored the emergence of the stoic notion of
cosmopolitanism.

Let me recall what Meleager of Gadara wrote in
the first century B.C.: "The only homeland, foreigner,
is the world we live in; a single Chaos has given birth
to all mortals." And also the famous statement by
Menander which we know through Terence's Latin
translation: "I am a man, and nothing human is foreign to me." For those intellectuals of the Hellenistic
period such as Zeno of Citium or Chrysippus living
beings are supported by the principle *oikeiosis* or conciliation; Cicero translated this as *commendatio* while
Seneca's word was *committo* . . . A first step-by-step
conciliation between the cosmos and living beings,
but also between every one and him or herself, such a
caritas generis humani (Cicero) was to end up in the
megapolis, the large polis, an ideal often articulated
during the imperial era, one that encompassed the
entire universe from citizens to the stars, including
Greeks and barbarians as well, slaves and free men.
That universalism of course rested on the pride of the
wise stoic, separated from the remainder of humanity
that was incapable of the same effort of reason and
wisdom; in utopic fashion this produced a new

strangeness—the strangeness of those who do not share in *our* reason. Stoicism thus appears more as an autarchy than as a way of thought that respects others. But its universalist breakthrough continued to make progress up to Locke, Shaftesbury, and Montesquieu, and, in my opinion, did not die out but rather took on a new orientation with the Freudian discovery of our intrinsic difference; let us know ourselves as unconscious, altered, other in order better to approach the universal otherness of the strangers that we are—for only strangeness is universal and such might be the post-Freudian expression of stoicism.

Caritas and Pilgrimage

A Jew from Tarsus in Cilicia, a polyglot, an untiring traveler of the eastern Mediterranean between the years A.D. 45 and 60, Paul was to change the small Jewish sect known as the Christian church into an *ecclesia.* The kinship between this new type of community and the stoic ideal of the *megapolis* has been noted. What has perhaps been less obvious is that by adding to the community of citizens in the *polis* another community—no longer a "political" one but a community of individuals who transcended their nationalities by means of a faith in the body of the risen Christ—Paul the stranger was addressing strangers. A Jew who spoke Greek and had rabbinical training, a Roman citizen and proud to be so, Saul/Paul crisscrossed Europe and especially its border provinces; often around synagogues, he spoke to marginal people: merchants, sailors, exiles, Jews at odds with orthodoxy, and women (Lydia or other "ladies of quality" as they are called in the Acts). The Pauline *ecclesia* thus became a community of foreigners for whom Paul's genius consists in finding a new "common denominator": "There is neither Greek nor Jew," but a "new creature," no more *laos* (Greek people) or *guer* (foreigner or Jewish "proselyte") but, through the suffering of those uprooted wanderers, identification with the passion and resurrection of Christ. Such identification, which was a genuine *therapy* offered by Paul for the disarray of foreigners in that era, is called *eucharist* and *ecclesia*.

Let us bow, in passing, to Paul's psychological and political sensitivity. No one can forget the excesses that the puristic and inquisitorial ecclesiastical institution inflicted upon heretics, that new variant of strangers, throughout the centuries. Nevertheless Paul's spirit would be seen again many times in the history of Christendom. Thus, Augustine's *civitas peregrina* advocated as the only state of freedom, against the state of oppression, that of pilgrimage: tearing oneself away from places to accomplish universal mutual assistance, but also tearing oneself away from any identity (including one's own) in order to accomplish subjective fulfillment in the boundlessness of *caritas*.

The discovery of "savages" from the Renaissance

up to recent colonialism has shown the narrowness and fragility of *caritas*'s boundaries. The fact remains, nonetheless, that lacking a more thorough analysis of the motivating forces that control our ties to others and to our own otherness, the Pauline and Augustinian messages remain a means of summoning people of goodwill against xenophobia and racism, as is demonstrated by the social activity in favor of immigration of Christian churches today.

Sovereign Because Doubly Impoverished

Far be it from me to sum up in one section the attitude toward foreigners on the part of Judaism, the other major ingredient of our culture. If it is true that the alliance with God constitutes the Jewish people as a chosen people (since Jacob and the departure from Egypt), and if it establishes the foundation for a sacred nationalism, it nevertheless provides for, in its very essence, a primal inscription of foreignness. That is what I have chosen to emphasize here, for it appeals to me personally and I believe it should be encouraged today in the political and religious ordeal experienced by the state of Israel. A foreign woman, Ruth the Moabite, crystallizes the tendency I have in mind.

It was forbidden to marry a foreigner, particularly a Moabite, for the people of the land of Moab were especially hostile to the Jews at the time of the Exodus. Now it happened that in a period of distress in

Judea a man named Elimelech left the country, settled in Moab, and his two sons married two Moabite princesses, Ruth and Orpah. After the men died Ruth and her mother-in-law Naomi returned to Judea, Ruth seemingly desirous to follow not only Naomi but also Naomi's God. Such acceptance continued when Ruth, after marrying Boaz, not without a few deviations from levirate rules, gave him an heir, Obed—he who "serves" God. Ruth's child indeed serves to further Boaz's lineage, to have Ruth be forgotten (the text no longer mentions her) in favor of her mother-in-law, to insure a bond between two peoples, and to found a lineage of kings; Obed was the "father of Isaiah, father of David." Thus it was that foreignness was inherent in Jewish royalty. Some blamed David for his foreign ancestry, others pointed out that the letter *dalet* in the royal name means "doubly impoverished," and that those who do not know how to read it should remember Ruth who reminds us that divine revelation requires a disparity, the welcoming of a radical otherness, the acknowledging of a foreignness that one would at first tend to consider the most degraded.

That meaning of Ruth's parable should not cause one to forget that, according to a strict interpretation of Judaic law, the "foreigner" (*guer*) is identical with the "proselyte": the same word stands for the two realities, as if the only foreigner one could imagine is one who accepted Jewish laws and customs. The history of the persecutions of which the Jewish people have been the victims accounts for such an assimilation of the "foreigner" to the "proselyte," who had a protective value for the Jewish community. It is true nevertheless that within a religious group, benevolence toward a foreigner depends on a precondition: acceptance of that group's dogmas signifies in fact that the foreigner as such has been absorbed and erased. While it was a shield against barbarian excesses during certain epochs, such a concept is no longer compatible with a contemporary attitude that claims the right to a difference and the dignity of every denomination as well as its relativity within the efforts of humankind to abolish absolute Truth in favor of more singular truths.

Rights of Man or Rights of the Citizen?

I would consequently like to end this brief historical journey by evoking two concepts of foreignness that we have inherited from the French Enlightenment, whose struggle against religious fanaticism of all kinds is well known. I shall nevertheless remind the reader that revolutionary terror was first directed against foreigners—and that there were many republican decrees (which I mentioned in *Strangers to Ourselves*) that promulgated a brutal persecution of foreigners in the name of nationalism; for the first time in the history of humanity the latter was raised to the level of a politico-economic, restrictive, and potentially totalitarian concept and reality.

By maintaining the distinction between human being and citizen, the 1789 *Declaration of the Rights of Man and Citizen* acknowledged its belonging to a historical moment: the sovereignty of the nation had just been asserted at the expense of the privileges of a state or class, and it was impossible to leap beyond that point into the unfolding of history. Nevertheless, one question cannot be avoided and Hannah Arendt has put it before us: what happens to people without nations, without territories—Russians, Poles, Jews? Are they human beings if they are not citizens? After criticizing Burke, who rejected the French *Declaration* because of its "abstraction" that would not have taken into account the national roots of English political thought, she implicitly agreed with him in the end: the *Declaration of the Rights of Man and Citizen* is considered too abstract, the Nazis would not have appreciated its abstraction, they allowed themselves to be seduced by more concrete realities, precisely national ones.

After having acknowledged the historical limitation and the moral danger the distinction between human being and citizen posited in the *Declaration* might lead to, I would nonetheless like to defend, in the final analysis, its appositeness. It would seem to me that to uphold a universal, transnational principle of Humanity that is distinct from the historical realities of nation and citizenship constitutes, on the one hand, a continuation of the Stoic and Augustinian legacy, of that ancient and Christian cosmopolitanism that finds its place among the most valuable assets of our civilization and that we henceforth must go back to and bring up to date. But above all and on the other hand, such upholding of a universality, of a symbolic dignity for the whole of humankind, appears to me as a rampart against a nationalist, regionalist, and religious fragmentation whose integrative contractions are only too visible today. Yes, let us have universality for the rights of man, provided we integrate in that universality not only the smug principle according to which "all men are brothers" but also that portion of conflict, hatred, violence, and destructiveness that for two centuries since the *Declaration* has ceaselessly been unloaded upon the realities of wars and fratricidal closeness and that the Freudian discovery of the unconscious tells us is a surely modifiable but yet constituent portion of the human psyche.

I shall go back for a few moments to the wealth of Enlightenment thought concerning foreigners and strangeness. Beyond the excesses of the revolutionary Reign of Terror two names need to be mentioned: Montesquieu (1689–1755) and Diderot (1713–1784).

The author of *The Spirit of the Laws* was one among those neoStoics who, as early as the seventeenth century, saw Europe as one: "Europe is but one nation made up of several, France and England need the opulence of Poland and Muscovy" (*Reflections on Uni-*

versal Monarchy). In his cosmopolitanism, however, he protected the *rights of man* beyond the *rights of the citizen,* concerned as he was to protect "privacy," "weakness," and "shyness," so that homogenous, uniform sociality would not erase them. He reached the following statement of how the individual and the different can be integrated in a higher whole that not only respects each of them but, one might almost say, gives them their requirements for existential difference:

"If I knew something useful to myself and detrimental to my family, I would reject it from my mind. If I knew something useful to my family but not to my homeland, I would try to forget it. If I knew something useful to my homeland and detrimental to Europe, or else useful to Europe and detrimental to Mankind, I would consider it a crime." [11]

With Diderot and *Rameau's Nephew* there merges, within the universalism of the Enlightenment, the acknowledgement of strangeness—call it "negativity," or "madness," or "art"—that will lead, by way of Hegel, himself a well-known commentator of *Rameau's Nephew,* to objectifying such a universal negative by means of the Freudian notion of the *unconscious.* Bizarre, playful, cynical, erotic, having a spasmodic body, an ironic, allusive, polyphonic, and often elliptic language, a critic of social mores but also of the philosophic reasoning of the reasonable "Myself," "He" in Diderot's text inserts strangeness into us. The

Nephew's "torn consciousness" (Hegel) is the culture that knows itself as such: knowing that we are at least double, like the Nephew, knowing that we are unconscious, we accomplish an essential step in culture. By mending that laceration, we shall attain absolute religion or spirit. I have, however, just mentioned some of the totalizing pitfalls involved. Let us then remain within the culture and endeavor, as did the Nephew, to recognize ourselves as strange in order better to appreciate the foreigners outside us instead of striving to bend them to the norms of our own repression.

Strangeness Within Ourselves: the Unconscious

To my knowledge, there has been no extensive study of Diderot and *Rameau's Nephew* as ancestors of Freud. It suits me to mention the relationship here, not only for the sake of ensuring a rhetorical transition but because the Nephew personifies—for the purposes of a narrative—the paradoxical logic that Freud discovered in the uncanny strangeness of our unconscious. [12] In the beginning was hatred, Freud said basically (contrary to the well-known biblical and evangelical statement), as he discovered that the human child differentiates itself from its mother through a rejection affect, through the scream of anger and hatred that accompanies it, and through the "no" sign as prototype of language and of all symbolism. To recognize the impetus of that hatred aroused by the other,

within our own psychic dramas of psychosexual indi-
viduation—that is what psychoanalysis leads us to. It
thus links its own adventure with the meditations
each one of us is called upon to engage in when
confronted with the fascination and horror that a
different being produces in us, such meditations being
prerequisite to any legal and political settlement of
the immigration problem.

Nowhere Is One More a Foreigner Than in France

After going along a path whose cultural and unconscious memory I should very much like you to have
discovered in yourselves, I wish to approach the national reality that I know best—the French reality—
in order to give a new impetus to our reflection on
identity and strangeness on the basis of that reality.

Nowhere is one *more* a foreigner than in France.
The coherence of the mosaic known as France, bonded
by royal and republican administrations as well as by
the *lycées* and the literary institution, rejects the notion of difference and sets aside for the foreigner a
solitary curiosity, the weird charms of which soon
prove to be a source of scorn. French chauvinism,
which ranges from 1793 to the Dreyfus case and even
to the Vichy regime of Marshal Pétain, embodies one
of the toughest variations, often not without subtlety,
of widespread nationalism—thus, today, the opposi-

tion to the foreigners' right to vote. If I claim, none-theless, that nowhere is one *better* as a foreigner than in France, this is because Montesquieu's message has not died out and is often propitious enough to change a social problem, such as immigration, into a politi-cal, legal, and ideological debate that involves the whole of society. *S.O.S. Racisme* is a French product, as is the so-called Committee of Wise Men that is studying the Nationality Code. Consequently, I was able to write to Harlem Désir to suggest that his friends ponder the social and moral values of the "body France" into which foreigners, whose right to vote we want them to obtain, wish to become inte-grated. For recognition of otherness is a right and a duty for everyone, French people as well as foreigners, and it is reasonable to ask foreigners to recognize and respect the strangeness of those who welcome them—French people in this instance (but also the Germans, the British, the Indians, and so forth). For there is otherness for all others, and it is precisely such exten-sion of otherness that Montesquieu invites us to re-spect by thinking of the social body as a guaranteed hierarchy of *private rights*, which he called *esprit gén-éral*. Give a place to foreigners in the "nation" under-stood as *esprit général*—such is, as I see it, the optimal version of integration and of the nation today.

The political right, which considers foreigners sim-ply as an additional strength or, on the contrary, as an economic hindrance, obliterates their symbolic values and function and does not raise that question. Inversely and symmetrically, by granting them a Promethean messianism that would have the power to resolve the deadlocks of the Old World, the left demagogically flatters the immigrants and runs down the national reality into which they hope to become integrated, leaving to the far right the easy privilege of appropriating to itself the wealth of our cultures, which are indeed ambivalent but fraught with libertarian potentialities.

Understood in such manner, a certain national idea that I trace back to Montesquieu's genius is at the same time affirmed as a space of freedom and dissolved in its own identity, eventually appearing as a texture of many singularities—confessional, linguistic, behavioral, sexual, and so forth.

That idea, with which I wholeheartedly agree, as it brings together the national and the cosmopolitan without for that matter erasing national boundaries—which remain a historical necessity for the coming century at least—runs headlong into a concept of the nation that I would describe as "mystical." Neither political, legal, nor confederalist, the emblem of which I take from Montesquieu, but on the contrary rooted in soil, blood, and language, that national idea, which emerges again with renewed strength in today's Eastern Europe, goes back, beyond German Romanticism and its Nazi exploitations, to the ambiguity of the great Herder (1744–1803). I am aware of his Augus-

tinian cosmopolitanism, his indebtedness to the Enlightenment, his warnings against the greater Ger-
many megalomania, as well as his essential contribution to the awakening of the folklore of national
cultures and of the social dignity of the peoples of
Central Europe; I also take good note of the differences that distinguish *Another Philosophy of History*
from *Ideas on the Philosophy of History of Mankind*.
Nonetheless, the secret notion of *Volksgeist*, one that
is intimate and indeed mystical (in the sense of *Gemüt*
and *Einfühlung*), appears to me as favoring hegemonic
claims (be they German, Hungarian, or Romanian)
and is a product of the same disease, with differences
that are simply quantitative and, one would hope,
consequences less catastrophic than those of the Third
Reich, wherever that ideology turns up. I would thus
assert that nationalism is neither "good" nor "bad,"
but that within the reality of national identities, which
cannot be transcended today or in a long time, I
would choose Montesquieu's *esprit général* over Herder's *Volksgeist*. [13]

Are Women Nationalists?

Women—I return to the Danaides who were the
starting point of Greek thought concerning foreigners—are particularly vulnerable to a possible support
of *Volksgeist*. The biological fate that causes us to be
the *site* of the species chains us to *space:* home, native

soil, motherland (*matrie*) (as I wish to say, instead of fatherland [*patrie*]). Worshipping the *national language* arouses a feeling of revenge and narcissistic satisfaction in a number of women, who are otherwise sexually, professionally, and politically humiliated and frustrated. The very recent studies that are beginning to be published on the underlying logic of Soviet society and of the transition period (that is already bitterly being called "catastroika") show to what extent a society based on the rudimentary satisfaction of survival *needs,* to the detriment of the *desires* for freedom, could encourage the regressive sado-masochist leanings of women and, without emancipating them at all, rely on them to create a stagnation, a parareligious support of the status quo crushing the elementary rights of the human person. Considerable watchfulness is thus needed in order to ward off that too facile symbiosis between nationalism and, if not "feminism," at least a certain conformist "maternalism" that lies dormant in every one of us and can turn women into accomplices of religious fundamentalisms and mystical nationalisms as they were of the Nazi mirage.

Allow me to preserve a tone that I do not consider somber but simply worried and, as such, embodying a piece of evidence pointing to the acute consciousness women are able to have of their role today. Gone are the days, in my opinion, of the complacency that blocked all criticism and self-criticism lest one strengthen "machismo" attitudes or "patriarchal" society. Foreign to the unisex commonality of men, everlasting irony of the community, as the sorrowful Hegel so aptly said, women today are called upon to share in the creation of new social groupings where, by *choice* rather than on account of *origin*, through lucidity rather than fate, we shall try to assure our children living spaces that, within ever tenacious national and identity-forging traditions, will respect the strangeness of each person within a lay community. Women have the luck and the responsibility of being boundary-subjects: body and thought, biology and language, personal identity and dissemination during childhood, origin and judgment, nation and world— more dramatically so than men are. It is not easy to avoid the snares of that condition, which could condemn us exclusively, through regression or flight from the superego, to one side or the other (nationalist or world-oriented militants).

But there are historical stakes involved in attempting to mesh our institutions with the demands of the polynational societies that are coming into being today, around us and with us. The maturity of the second sex will be judged in coming years according to its ability to modify the nation in the face of foreigners, to orient foreigners confronting the nation toward a still unforeseeable conception of a polyvalent community. Before reaching that moment, which will remain for yet a long time a distant ideal, we have a generative utopian thought—a world without foreigners.

A Mediterranean Melting Pot

Facing the melting pot that the Mediterranean community is going to become with the flow of increasing population rates as early as the year 2000, the matter of Arabian immigration in France is the major problem that arises when one considers the coexistence of French people and foreigners today. The 1990–1991 crisis in the Gulf has already aggravated it and could well give a dramatic turn to that integration or confrontation. The French population is subjected to a twofold humiliation: First there is the interior impact of immigration, which often makes it feel as though it had to give up traditional values, including the values of freedom and culture that were obtained at the cost of long and painful struggles (why accept [that daughters of Maghrebin immigrants wear] the Muslim scarf [to school]?[14] Why change spelling?— while the French secular tradition asserts women's freedom and is proud of an education system that gives one access to the linguistic subtleties of Molière and Proust); then there is the exterior impact of tomorrow's broadened Europe (why should the Deutsche Mark's performance bring about the decline of French-speaking communities and of French culture generally in Eastern Europe, for instance?). That involves a

breach of the national image and it corresponds, on
the individual level, to the good image of itself that
the child makes up with the help of the ego ideal and
the parental superego, allowing it to grow up and
acquire its culture—or, on the contrary, when that
good image is damaged, leads it into depression and
inhibition. Le Pen's nationalism takes advantage of
such depression and inhibition, and I am grieved to
have heard on many occasions, left-wing intellectuals, for the sake of a misunderstood cosmopolitanism, sell off French national values, including and
often mainly the values of the Enlightenment, considered once more—and wrongly so—to be too French
or too unaware of the particularities of others. If France,
along with other countries of the European south such
as Spain and Italy (but perhaps even more actively
than they because of its contentious intellectual tradition), is to be the leaven of a Mediterranean peace
and of a new polynational set of Mediterranean nations this can be accomplished, in my opinion, on
the basis of enriched and expanded secular values,
which were achieved by the Enlightenment as I have
just evoked them. To what libertarian, cultural, professional, or other advantage would a Muslim wish to
join the French community, the southern European
community (that harbors particularities to be distin-
guished from those of the north), and eventually the
European community? We must be more positive—I
might say more aggressive—as we bring our culture to

the fore; and intellectuals are those who must be
asked for such a contribution if we want the Mediterranean peace not to be a repetition of Rome's fall as
we experience a feeling of guilt in the face of an influx
of humiliated and demanding Arabian masses. Let us
not be ashamed of European and particularly French
culture, for it is by developing it critically that we
have a chance to have foreigners recognize us as being
foreigners all, with the same right of mutual respect.

Far be it from me to claim a cultural hierarchy and
much less so the supremacy of one over the others.
Nonetheless, we must note that as far as recognizing
the other is concerned—the other as different, as
foreign—Western culture has, with its Greek, Jewish,
and Christian components, traveled a road as difficult, as strewn with risks and pitfalls, errors and crimes,
as in other respects it bears uneasy meditations and
promises that await their individual and social fulfillment. That await us.

The French National Idea

In France, where ridicule kills, nationalism is in bad
taste and patriotism downright trashy. Nevertheless,
foreigners experience more strongly than elsewhere
the scorn and rejection that is inflicted upon them by
a civilization sure of itself and the more tensed up as
it feels humiliated by American supremacy, German
competition, and the "invasion" from the Maghreb.

"I am against Le Pen," a young boy asserted during a Parisian dinner party, knowing it would please his parents' enlightened guests. "So you like foreigners," countered a guest eager to elucidate matters. The parents were silent, embarrassed. "Well?"—"Oh, foreigners, let's forget about them," the child concluded to the accompaniment of strained laughter. That is what we have come to. After Iraq, Kuwait, America, Romania, Albania, and a few others, without mentioning the immigrants in our neighborhoods, France withdraws into itself, aloof, discreet, but anxious to assert its values. The Nation is not dead, and who would blame it for that?

The disarray as to identity, which just recently added to the membership and the votes of the National Front, has henceforth found a positive countenance: one need only look and read in order to notice the proud return of the eighteenth century, a taste for French painting, the Cyrano de Bergerac syndrome, if not matters of spelling or the effective electronics of our Jaguars in the Gulf, and to be persuaded that the "consensus" actually seeks, and finds, its true object in the nation.

In the face of a resurgence of the French national spirit, and without being unaware of its dangers and of the difficulty of living in France as a foreigner, I nevertheless assert that there exists a French national idea that can make up the *optimal rendition* of the nation in the contemporary world. Quite the opposite of the "spirit of the people" (*Volksgeist*), whose origins have been traced back to the ambiguities of the great Herder and that is mystically rooted in the soil, the blood, and the genius of the language, the French national idea, which draws its inspiration from the Enlightenment and is embodied in the French Republic, is achieved in a *legal and political pact* between free and equal individuals. If it be true that it thus causes the *sacred* to be absorbed by the *national* identified with the *political,* it does not do so only to ensure the most rational conditions for the development of capitalism, but also and above all put forward its dynamics toward accomplishing the rights of man. [15]

Though heir to the eighteenth century and the founding principles of the French Republic, the "nation in the French style" is not an already accomplished, perfected idea, much less a reality that one would simply need to actualize again or to propagate. It remains to be put together in agreement with the contemporary demands of France and the world.

A Transitional Logic

Furthermore, its "contractual" aspect, which many writers have emphasized, does not exhaust its features. The French national idea seems to me to be endowed with two other qualities that make it remarkably topical: it is *transitional* and it is *cultural.*

The quotation from Montesquieu's *Thoughts* (see

above p. 28) refers indeed to a series of sets that, from the individual to the family, from the country to Europe and to the world, respects the particular if, and only if, it is integrated into another particular, of greater magnitude, but that at the same time guarantees the existence of the previous one and lifts it up to respecting new differences that it might tend to censor if it were not for that logic. The nation as a *series of differences* consequently demands that particular rights be highlighted (those of individuals, with their behavioral or sexual peculiarities; those of families, with the couples' new modes of living together or not together; those of ethnic groups, with their customs, beliefs, religions) while they are being absorbed into the lay aggregate of the nation where such differences, which are acknowledged, nevertheless give way before the "general interest," the *esprit général* favored by Montesquieu. Hence open-ended, such a transitional nation is also spread open in the direction of sets that acknowledge and limit it for the sake of another general interest—the general interest of Europe and of the world.

The transitional object—any child's indispensable fetish, which condenses its own evolving image with that of its mother from whom it is beginning to grow away—constitutes that area of play, freedom, and creation that guarantees our access to speech, desires, and knowledge. There are mothers (as well as "motherlands" and "fatherlands") who prevent the creation of a transitional object; there are children who are unable to use it. As a counterpoint to that psychoanalytical account, let us give thought to the transitional nation that offers its identifying (therefore reassuring) space, as transitive as it is transitory (therefore open, uninhibiting, and creative), for the benefit of contemporary subjects: indomitable individuals, touchy citizens, and potential cosmopolitans.

Consequently, there are those who fear to see the French version of the nation decline, since the supremacy it gives to individual rights changes into egotism and can weaken the convivial bond, as in the Scandinavian mode or the votary people's genius, as in the German style. I maintain, on the contrary, that such a seeming threat is a necessity and a trump card for the nation as transitional reality.

For in the serial logic of concord, the fate of the nation, absolute because it is transitive, is to insure the best accomplishment of men and women, natives and foreigners, within those articulated groupings (nations, Europe or other geographico-historical units, and so forth) not only because this is forced upon us by the worldwide sway of the economy but also, morally speaking, because it is our duty to reconcile the desires of the most efficient individuals and nations with the needs of the most disadvantaged individuals and nations. With respect to such a dynamics, national unity is a necessary and relative cohesion: thus the assertion of persons, of their technical specializations, of their moral or esthetic abilities, is already a fact within the national framework and is *immediately taken over* by international associations, particularly professional ones, where the competition with others refines one's singularity in spite of and beyond the tendency to step back into a universal similarity. The fear that the idea of the nation might be "weakened" is perhaps a nostalgic, melancholy interpretation of that transitional logic characteristic of the French national idea in its effort to reconcile the individual, the national, and the transnational; for if it is true that such a concept was substituted for the sacred, which merged monarchy and religion in the Ancien Régime, its logic demands that, on account of its transitional character, the nation be potentially stripped of the sacral aspects of its totality to the advantage of the greatest growth of its members.

A Totally Discoursive Being

Finally, welded as it is by culture and its institutions—from Benedictine and Jesuit schools to state schools, from the French Academy to the Collège de France, from the worship of rhetorics to literary prizes—the nation in its French style is a highly symbolic body. Art and literature are the signs of recognition with which the most unassuming citizen identifies. "Literature plays a considerable part in the consciousness France acquires of itself and its civilization. No other nation grants it comparable place. Only in France does the entire nation consider literature to be the representative expression of its fate," Ernst Robert Curtius wrote in 1930. The result is a national stability (devotion to the literary tradition) as well as a plasticity (taste for stylistic inventiveness) that brings about admiration and irritation on the part of onlookers: "The most brilliant and most dangerous of European nations, and in the best position to become by turns an object of admiration, hatred, pity, terror, but never of indifference" (Alexis de Tocqueville).

Thus equating the national and the cultural, a process that often deteriorates in causing elitism and meritocracy at the expense of solidarity nevertheless has the advantage of stimulating the *shaping* and *ideating* of identification instincts, with the result that a distance (that is a sublimation) is set up from their dominating and persecuting pressures. Consequently, national literature could, in France, become not the expression of the people's enigmatic intimacy but a charmed space where irony merges with seriousness in order to lay out and break up the changing outlines of the totally discursive being, which, when all is said and done, constitutes the French nation. To write in French, to write a fiction in French, as I have done with *The Samurai* and *The Old Man and the Wolves*, is at the same time an acknowledgement of the fact that a nation (the French one) is a language act and an attempt to inscribe on it other sensitivities, other

experiences, and strangenesses apt to extend its pur-
suit of universality.

Self-Deprecation and Self-Hatred

Can such a contractual, transitional, and cultural nation survive the rise of romantic or even integrating
nationalism that is shaking Eastern Europe under the
appearance of legitimate democratic demands[16] and
coincides with the religious expansionism in many
third world countries (the Arab "nation," for instance—a mythical product of Muslim religion, beyond cultural, economic, and political specificities)?
You don't think it can?

That kind of pessimism would have the benefit of
recognizing the violence of identifying drives that are
supported by death drive. But it also has the disadvan-
tage of sanctioning, in the last analysis, the narrow
nationalisms that reflect those drives. From Edmund
Burke to Hannah Arendt, even political analysts allow themselves to be captivated by the mystical calls
of the *Volk* (which would cast a spell on the masses)
far more than they would be attracted by the "abstraction" ascribed to the French national model stemming
from the Enlightenment. If, however, the masses favor fascism, is that a reason to give up the fight? Let
us, rather, take more seriously the *violence* of the
desire to be different.

It is indeed to be feared that a time of nationalist

pretension and conflicts between nations that consider themselves sacred threatens some sections of
Europe and especially the developing countries. The
French-style contractual, transitional, and cultural
nation will nonetheless remain a goal that French
society henceforth has the economic and political
maturity to work out for itself as well as keeping it
alive for the rest of the world. For later? Why not.
Let an outsider be allowed to share that hope.

But after all, is not the "French model's" universalism a historical and regional mirage, the pure product
of an enlightened utopia for a limited portion of Europe, one that does not correspond with the development of peoples who have been awakened today on
the basis of another history, other mental attitudes?

The critical mind of French intellectuals often ex-
cels in self-deprecation and self-hatred. When they
do not take aim at themselves and proclaim their own
death, their national tradition—and especially the
Enlightenment—become their privileged objects of
destruction. There are countless publications and
conferences that "prove" the natural filiation leading
from the Encyclopedia to the Third Republic and
colonialism, to Nazism and Stalinism. The time has
perhaps come for pursuing a critique of the national
tradition without selling off its assets. Let us ask, for
instance, where else one might find a theory and a
policy more concerned with respect for the *other*,
more watchful of citizen's rights (women and foreigners included, in spite of blunders and crimes), more

concerned with individual strangeness, in the midst of a national mobility?

The right of foreigners to be integrated is a right to participate in this contractual, transitional, and cultural nation. Old-stock Frenchmen are not conscious of it? It would be proper to give that consciousness back to them, to create it if need be, on the basis of their tradition and its necessary transformation by current events. Can one be sure that even foreigners, who are asking for "integration," are aware of and appreciate that French *esprit général* in which they seemingly wish to take their place? What are the personal, symbolic, political benefits that they expect from the French nation? It is possible that the "abstract" advantages of French universalism may prove to be superior to the "concrete" benefits of a Muslim scarf, for instance. In any case, let us begin by asking the question, as I wrote to Harlem Désir, without false humility on the part of the hosts, without false overvaluation of the immigrants' virtues.

For, among the foreigners that we all are (within ourselves and in relation to others), such an exchange can in the future amplify and enrich the French idea of the nation. It is a fragile idea but nevertheless one bearing a chance of incomparable liberty, one that today happens to be challenged by wounded, therefore aggressive, nationalisms of Eastern Europe and the Mediterranean, but one that might be, tomorrow, a resource in the search for new forms of community among individuals that are different and free.

Open Letter to Harlem Désir

February 24, 1990

Dear Harlem Désir,

I fear that the lateness of the hour and short time devoted to the discussion did not allow me to clarify my statements concerning the nation today. That is what I should like to do, if only briefly, by means of this "open letter," which is intended for you and those who took part in the *Forum*. [1]

No, I do not believe that henceforth the future can no longer be set within the national framework. No, I do not count myself among those who consider that to insist on what is "national" is inevitably to impose, indirectly, racial values.

As a foreigner and a cosmopolitan (as I tried to explain in *Strangers*

49

to Ourselves [Columbia University Press, 1991]) I insist on such an atopic (foreignness) and utopic (a concord of people without foreigners, hence without nations) position as a means to stimulate and update the discussion on the meaning of the "national" today. For I am convinced that contemporary French and European history, and even more so that of the rest of the world, imposes, for a *long while,* the necessity to think of the *nation* in terms of new, flexible concepts because it is within and through the nation that the economic, political, and cultural future of the coming century will be played out.

Of course, Freud has demonstrated to what extent the conglomeration of men and women into sets is oppressive and death-bearing. "Society is founded on a common crime," he wrote in *Totem and Taboo,* and the exclusion of "others," which binds the identity of a clan, a sect, a party, or a nation, is equally the source of the pleasure of identification ("this is what *we* are, therefore it is what *I* am") and of barbaric persecution ("that is foreign to me, therefore I throw it out, hunt it down, or massacre it"). The complex relationships between cause and effect that govern social groups obviously do not coincide with the laws of the unconscious regarding a subject, but these unconscious determinations remain a constituent part, an essential one, of social and therefore national dynamics.

Indeed, I am convinced that, in the long run, only

a thorough investigation of our remarkable relationship with both the *other* and *strangeness within ourselves* can lead people to give up hunting for the
scapegoat outside their group, a search that allows
them to withdraw into their own "sanctum" thus
purified: is not the worship of one's "very own," of
which the "national" is the collective configuration,
the *common denominator* that we imagine we have as
"our own," precisely, along with other "own and
proper" people like us?

Nevertheless, such an ethical course suggested by
psychoanalysis but also, in different fashion, by *contemporary philosophy*—devoted as it is to analyzing singularity and the right to anomaly as the end and surpass-
ing of the rights of man—as well as *literature*, which
is written as a defense of the dignity of the strange—
that ethical course, then, which can develop patient,
complex discourses, involving everyone's meditation,
does not exonerate us, quite the contrary, from putting the "national" back into question:

"Is there a way of thinking politically about the
"national" that does not degenerate into an exclu-
sory, murderous racism, without at the same time
dissolving into an all-encompassing feeling of "S.O.S.-
Absolute Brotherhood" and providing, for the span of
an evening, all who represent groups (historical identities that have been respectively persecuted and persecuting) with the delight of being on a boundless
ocean?"

The question ensues from the modern political necessity that challenges the retrograde, racial, or simply casual forms of nationalism, but it demands an optimal definition of the "national," on two accounts: as guarantee for the identification pride of individuals and groups and as a historically indispensable transition for the insertion of national entities inherited from the past into higher political and economic wholes.

National pride is comparable, from a psychological standpoint, to the *good narcissistic image* that the child gets from its mother and proceeds, through the intersecting play of identification demands emanating from both parents, to elaborate into an ego ideal. By not being aware of, underestimating, or degrading such a narcissistic image or ego ideal, one humiliates and lays subject or group open to *depression.* What are the signs of this? Idleness, withdrawal from communication, and any participation in collective projects and representations. Or else, as a counteraction, in solidary fashion, the narcissistic excitement of rediscovering strengthened, superegotic, hyperbolic "ideals," of which the aggressive, paranoid excesses are well known. Between suicide and barbarity, there is not much leeway for one—individual or nation—who has been demeaned by losing the optimal narcissistic image, the regulating ego ideal.

But where is the *optimal* located? That is the most difficult aspect of the question.

We have no choice here but to abandon psychoanalytic references and turn to political sociology. Far be it from me to suggest *a* model, much less so *the* optimal national model. I shall merely turn to a line of reasoning that put its stamp on French political thought during the Enlightenment and attempt to draw from it a few lessons for the national problem today.

My starting point will be Montesquieu, who has been the object of many commentaries and preemptions, as well as a major reference for thinkers as dissimilar as Robert Aron and Louis Althusser (to mention only two recent French theoreticians).[2] I hope I shall be forgiven for alluding to his huge work only briefly and schematically within the laconic framework of this letter and the scope of our present discussion.

I am among those who dread and reject the notion of *Volksgeist*, "spirit of the people," which stems from a line of thinkers that includes Herder and Hegel. I know that it is not foolishly racial in the one or simply absolutist and totalizing in the other. Herder, the folklorist, was a translator and his universalism—inherited from the stoics (like that of Montesquieu, by the way), Augustinian Christianity, and the universalism of the Enlightenment—went against national hegemony—above all against German supremacy. The fact remains, nevertheless, that the romantic interpretation and the Nazi implementation of the *Volks-*

geist cause me to be perplexed by the nationalistic boom among Eastern European peoples today; a boom that expresses itself through the same laudatory phrases such as eternal memory, linguistic genius, ethnic purity, and an identifying superego, all the more aggressive as these peoples were humiliated.

A libertarian mainspring at the beginning, that sort of nationalism, more or less consciously dependent on the *Volksgeist,* changes—only too rapidly as one can see—into a repressive force aimed at *other* peoples and extolling *one's own.* Is history about to resume its gruesome course, one that, after Napoleon's conquests, changed the surge of French-inspired revolutionary universalism on the continent into a nationalism that was revivalist at first but nevertheless ended up in Balkanizing the cultural, political, and economic forces of European peoples, who were thus exposed to the dominance of the strongest hegemonist?

But let me return to Montesquieu, to Book XIX, chapter 4, in *The Spirit of the Laws:*

"Human beings are ruled by several things: climate, religion, laws, principles of government, examples of things past, customs, manners; as a result, an *esprit général* is constituted."[3]

I should like to contrast that *esprit général* with the *Volksgeist.* Far from being an abstract ideality (it will be remembered that, from Edmund Burke to Hannah

Arendt, such was the main complaint against the French Revolution and the Enlightenment), the *esprit général* according to Montesquieu had the threefold advantage of reformulating the *national whole* as:

1. A *historical* identity.
2. A *layering* of very concrete and very diverse causalities (climate, religions, past, laws, customs, manners, and so forth).
3. A possibility of *going beyond* the political groups thus conceived as sharing an *esprit général* and into higher entities set forth by a spirit of concord and economic development: "Europe is no more than a nation made up of several others, France and England need the richness of Poland and Muscovy as one of their provinces needs the others . . ."[4]

Neither the legislative, nor the political, nor the national may assume, in the flexibility of that reasoning, the place of the "last recourse" so dear to our simplifying thoughts. On the contrary, the different levels of social reality are reintegrated into the *esprit général* without being absorbed; and this is accomplished, quite obviously, under the influence of the English model,[5] but also, in very original fashion, through the synthesizing power of the French philosopher's thought.

Consequently, we may define the *national* as being:

1. A *historical identity* with relative *steadiness* (the tradition) and an always prevailing *instability* in a given topicality (subject to evolution).

2. Endowed with a *logical multiplicity* whose diversity is to be maintained without the possibility of having one social (logical) stratum dominate the others. Thus, laws determine the citizens' actions but non-laws determine morals (inner behavior) and manners (outer behavior). Taking this social polylogics into account implies extending the *private* domain, but also and consequently that of *private law*,[6] by means of which legislators guarantee the free exercise of morals and manners, which, it is believed, and in reverse fashion, softens the very practice of legislators and causes the *general* (that is, the national as determined by legislation) to be put in concrete form in the *particular* (to guarantee individual freedoms in the bosom of, should I say, the "nation"?—or rather the *esprit général*). Thus, not only is the rigidity of a steadying, biological, totalizing, age-old, and motionless *national* concept set aside (after its existence has been recognized, particularly under the guise of our dependence on climate), but the very notion of *citizenship* becomes relative:

> "Men, in such a nation, would be confed-
> erates rather than citizens."[7]

I should like to argue that the nation as *esprit
général* (with the heterogeneous, dynamic, and "confederate" meaning that Montesquieu gives to a political group) is one of the most prestigious creations of
French political thought. Conceivably, it is a difficult
one to actualize and even more difficult to administer.
As the liberal empiricist Robert Aron foresaw, in
pragmatic fashion, the *esprit général* could be realized
by means of a clever alternation between the *political*
and the *national, dynamics* and *inertia* (might one say
today, between "citizenship" and "nationality"?). Such
an administrative interpretation of Montesquieu is
not without cleverness. It seems, nevertheless, that
the philosopher of the Enlightenment had elaborated
a higher perception of the national presence, one that
avoided isolating, on the one hand, abstract and evo-
lutive politics (citizenship) and, on the other, the
weighty, deterministic national (nationality); but he
suggested a concept, specifically his own and French,
involving the integration, without a leveling process,
of the different layers of social reality into the political and/or national unity.

It is up to specialists in political thought, and particularly Montesquieu's, to proceed with such clarifi-
cations.

As for me, I shall limit myself to the following brief

indications—without ignoring the ambiguities and the totalizing, or even totalitarian, uses that Montesquieu's thought is also open to, I would abandon his hierarchies and keep only his heterogeneities—in order to return to their consequences for the contemporary scene.

If the common denominator of the French nation is to be or could be the *esprit général* with Montesquieu's meaning, three major questions are to be asked:

1. What do we mean, today, when we say that French national identity is *historical?*
2. Consequently, what do we mean when we say that civil society is *manifold:* is it a concordance, a "confederation" of private rights?
3. How does one work out the fitting together of such different identities and social layers within groups where they would submit to a balance between *esprit général* and *private* concerns?

First, taking into account the historical nature of the French national identity demands a serious assessment of *traditional national memory:* the "customs of France" (Montesquieu), its *entire* religious history (Catholic, Protestant, Jewish, Muslim) and transcending that history during the Enlightenment when, precisely, one could think of the "nation" as having an *esprit général.* Valorizing this lay component—unfairly disparaged to the advantage of the particular-isms it might have neglected, in reality or in imagi-nation—is imperative if one wishes to raise the con-cept of nation beyond its regressive, exclusionary, integrative, or racial pitfalls.

It is the role of political parties and the media to initiate *schools* and *programs* to recall and give back value to such a tradition—in the eyes of French na-tionals to begin with. What is involved, in short, is giving them back their own history in a shape that would be most worthy of a complex national affirma-tion that, as nowhere else in the world, was able to compel recognition so as better to go beyond itself; for there is no way for an identity to go beyond itself without first asserting itself in satisfactory fashion. Let us again read Montesquieu: "Love for one's country leads to good behavior, and good behavior leads to love for one's country. The less we are able to assuage our individual passions, the more we engage in gen-eral ones."[8] Such a love for the "general," dependent on frustration, is characteristic of religious orders but not of the nation; the latter has heterogeneous com-ponents and causalities, which are called *esprit général* and demand that "love for the country" or group be enhanced in order to be transcended.

At the same time, a bold assessment is called for, without any false sense of propriety haunted by the fear of foundering in patriotic ridicule: one needs to examine the *twofold shock* presently being undergone by the national French customs due to the tide of immigration inside of France's territorial boundaries and to a confrontation with other European nations in a broadened concept of Europe.

Opening the discussion on those matters, with a broad participation and active interpretation on the part of intellectuals and political leaders, might prevent lamentations and feelings of fear or national defeatism from becoming ossified and mute and then being harnessed through the fanatical delectation of flatly nationalist and racial ideologies.

It is time, however, also to ask immigrant people what motivated them (beyond economic opportunities and approximate knowledge of the language propagated by colonialism) to choose the French community with its historical memory and traditions as the welcoming lands. The respect for immigrants should not erase the gratitude due the welcoming host. Only a misguided concern for Third World populations could prevent parties of the left from expressing that point, while those of the right were incapable of conceiving it, caught as they are in the symbolic underestimation of immigration that brings it down to a simple economic contribution (or hindrance). In other words, what does each immigrant community contribute to the lay concept of *national spirit as esprit général* reached by the French Enlightenment? Do those communities recognize that *esprit général* or not? What do they expect from that *national spirit*, which is to the credit of the country they are calling on to resolve their *contradictions and concrete needs,* and how do they wish to enrich it without denying it?

Should not foreigners' indispensable right to vote and their access to French nationality go through a pedagogical, mediatized, and political process opening up that question? For, without it, how shall we manage to have the citizens of that historically mobile group known as France today be something else than selfish people withdrawn into their own common denominators, more or less integration-minded or even death-bearing, and become "confederates" in the *esprit général?*

Second, the manifoldness of civil society that constitutes the indissociable facet of the *esprit général* and prevents it from freezing into an empty abstraction is the extraordinary ability to valorize and guarantee everyone's "customs" and "manners." The vast domain of the *private,* the land of welcome of individual, concrete freedoms, is thus immediately included in the *esprit général* that must guarantee through law and economy the private practice of religious, sexual, moral, and educational differences relating to the mindset and customs of the confederate citizens. Simultaneously, while the *private* is thus guaranteed, one is committed to respect the *esprit général* in the bosom of which there is a place for its own expansion, without for that matter hindering the "privacy" of the other communities that are included in the same *esprit général*. Respect for the *neutrality* of educational, medical, and similar spheres, as well as those of legal and political representation, should be the counterpart of that private practice of customs and manners guaranteed by the *esprit général*, to the richness of which these various particularities contribute.

Most of these remarks match principles accepted by French secularism. If one tends to reject them as abstract or not in keeping with the new national situation, it is because an inflexible comprehension of secularism has often pushed back into the darkness of "relics" or "archaism" those customs, morals, and manners that perhaps do not make citizens but profoundly shape human beings. Rejection also comes from underestimating—for various political and philosophical reasons—the inherent wealth of the Enlightenment's secularism, which should still be a wellspring for a political thought concerned with responding to integrating barbarians and the *Volksgeist*'s appropriating and authoritarian calls. Acknowledging and guaranteeing the *private* (I repeat: mores, customs, manners, religions) within the *esprit général* indeed makes up that series of *counterforces* that prevent erasing the national within the hegemony of abstract politics as well as devouring political space (the legislative separated from the executive) through an identifying nationalist obsession. Montesquieu again: "The duty of the citizen is a crime when it makes one forget the duty of man."[9] (A reminder: in the context of mores, customs, memory, history, climatic or other determinism, and so forth.)

Finally, and in conclusion to what precedes, I should like to suggest that the following statement be engraved on the walls of all schools and political institutions; commented and elaborated upon, it could become a touchstone for anyone wishing to participate in the French nation understood as an *esprit général*—a set of private freedoms liable to be included in larger sets:

"If I knew something useful to myself and detrimental to my family, I would reject it from my mind. If I knew something useful to my family, but not to my homeland, I would try to forget it. If I knew something useful to my homeland and detrimental to Europe, or else useful to Europe and detrimental to mankind, I would consider it a crime.[10]

The identities and the "common denominators" are acknowledged here, but one avoids their morbid contortion by placing them, without erasing them, in a polyphonic community that is today called France. Tomorrow, perhaps, if the *esprit général* wins over the *Volksgeist*, such a polyphonic community could be named Europe.

Forgive me for insisting on sharing that two-centuries-old thought and supposing it workable, with the necessarily concrete modifications that the French national situation makes necessary today.

Rest assured, dear Harlem Désir, of my
friendly feelings.
Julia Kristeva

P.S. I should like to invite, for the forthcoming meeting at which you suggested I might discuss the points of this letter, J. P. Dollé, whom we should, I am sure, be happy to hear talk about *The Fragrance of France,* and also Julien Dray, Roland Castro, and Philippe Sollers, who are all heedful of the contemporary fate of the "national." [11]

The Nation and the Word

At a time when mediocrity tempts one
from all sides I should act for the sake
of greatness.

—Charles de Gaulle

I live in France and I am a French
citizen thanks to de Gaulle. Such
an assertion, which one might
think pathetically contaminated by
Gaullish pomposity, nevertheless
conveys no more than stark reality. As early as 1963, a political
offensive toward Eastern Europe was
begun, conflicting with the Western allies and aiming at a détente
"among Europeans from the Atlantic to the Urals" in order to
remove "the violence [inherent in]
German problems." In calling upon
France to "carry out in the center

65

of things a policy that would be global in scope," de
Gaulle had already abolished the Berlin wall in this
blueprint for Europe that, within the past few months
(that is, sixteen years after the following text was
written), is taking shape before our very eyes:

"We must [. . .] consider the day when, perhaps,
in Warsaw, Prague, Pankow, Budapest, Bucharest,
Sofia, Belgrade, Tirana, Moscow, the totalitarian
Communist regime that is still able to constrain its
imprisoned people would gradually undergo an evolution reconcilable with our own transformation. Then,
the prospects worthy of its resources and capabilities
would be open to the whole of Europe."

Paternalistic toward Eastern Europe, as he was with
everyone? Of course. I have heard him say in Poland,
"[France] hopes that you will see farther ahead, on a
somewhat larger scale perhaps [. . .] You see what I
mean?" (1967). They were seeing it, and everyone
saw indeed: *Solidarity.*

And yet I was among those who, in 1968, from
Denfert-Rochereau to the Gare Saint-Lazare,[1] chanted,
"de Gaulle, resign," "Ten years, that's enough," "the
pigsty, that's him," and other crackpot and parricidal
catchphrases. Sartre was delighted, and so were all of
us along with him: the frogs no longer called for a
king, the rebellious, sovereign masses that they were
finally rose to throw him out. Supposing that another
de Gaulle might turn up, I am sure that ten years later
(or thirty) I would follow the same path.

But what do the people want anyway? A leader they can love and take issue with? A savior who humiliates them and allows them to humiliate him in turn?

De Gaulle was neither a monarch (who has nothing to do: "In the position where God has placed you, be what you are, Madame!" he challenged the queen of England), nor an administrator of political parties (whose hostage he constantly feared he might become); he began by redefining the *domain of the political*. He situated it on the boundary between *unconscious desires* for identity and power (that religion and psychology are fighting over) and *circumstances* (that are ruled by laws, force, diplomacy, and inevitably economics, which was not his strong point). Conceived in such a manner, the political became concretized during the twentieth century in the idea of *nation*. De Gaulle undertook to achieve it through the power of the *symbolic:* a thoroughly Christian revival of the primacy of the Word in order to "solidify" public opinion ("According to my way of proceeding, I think it appropriate to solidify public opinion."). Ever since the radio appeal of June 18, 1940, through the fantastic appearances on television during the Algerian war, and including the frequent resort to referenda, what was obvious was the assertion of personal power. At the same time there unfolded a passion for rhetorics over a reality that had been darkened by two world wars and colonization: the nation.

One could argue over the medieval or romantic coloring the idea of *nation* was imbued with by de Gaulle: a compact of faith and love ("I do not believe any human love has inspired more numerous and also more resilient devotions"), which, he told an astonished John Foster Dulles, is more important than the ideological conflict opposing the free world to communism. And again, "There will be no Western world," whereas where nations are concerned—there is no doubt about their existence . . . Starting from there, he decolonized the French Empire and undertook his march from the Atlantic to the Ural mountains, going on to Beijing. One cannot but recognize that today de Gaulle's concept of the nation has prevailed and is far from being exhausted. In fact, the time has come to combine it with a requirement for *integration* inside and outside of its borders. Who would be able to carry that out without breaking the nation but rather in order to transport it beyond itself? That is the question: the answer requires a de Gaulle who would have reread Montesquieu.

On account of the development from the guillotine to the separation of church and state, the political function has found itself lacking in symbolic dignity. Thus, removing it from its pedestal opened the way for democracy just as it facilitated wheeling and dealing and corruptions. The problem of the twentieth century was and remains the rehabilitation of the political. An impossible task? A useless task? Hitler and Stalin perverted the project into a deathly totalitarianism. The collapse of communism in Eastern Europe, which calls into question, beyond socialism, the very basis of the democratic governments that stemmed from the French Revolution, demands that one rethink that basis so that the twenty-first century not be the reactional domain of fundamentalisms, religious illusions, and ethnic wars.

Neither Führer, nor Communist Generalissimo, nor Pope, de Gaulle was simply a Catholic general unlike any other. As it turned out he was the only one, with his "popular monarchy," to offer not a "model" (one can only sink into mediocrity when imitating the great Charles Lackland who speaks to *himself* when addressing a France that he is. Thus, on June 18th, 1940: "In the name of France, I positively call upon you as follows: [. . .] arise!" And later: "At this moment, the worst in her history, it was up to me to take on France."), but a political attitude that regained the pride and joy of the Symbol, as well as an efficient hold on human beings who were led to make history. How did he do it?

By means of worshipping the Nation as a living and evolutionary unit and by anchoring his action on people's conscience in the radiance of the Word that gives access to each one's unconscious: *de Gaulle has succeeded where the paranoid fails.*

Freud alone claimed a success of that sort (*Letter to*

Ferenczi, October 6, 1910). But the psychoanalyst had allowed himself other means: lifting prohibitions, burrowing into words and desires, leading each person to his or her truths and limitations. The technique used by *Colonel Motor* or the *Connétable*[2] was quite different—restoring, daring, blunt; but what a style!

De Gaulle had understood that regicide peoples were also, and more so than others, orphaned peoples. On his own, he imposed a persona whose aura reached its peak in discourse, as solace for wounded ego ideal and superego. For, in individuals as well as human groups, the ego ideal and the superego, who are our tyrants, nevertheless guarantee identity and regulate actions. He toyed with that potential tyranny of the Ideal, took his chances, but eventually reaped its advantages. Against depression, he proposed lofty aims that provided for a national temperament and mass jouissance. Consequently, the offended parties outshone themselves, rediscovered a land, remade a state, freed their former slaves ("those from the Algerian mountains"), taught a thing or two to the workers of Leningrad ("Keep it up . . ."), and "recognized" (!) the Chinese, rebelled in the Sorbonne but again found euphoria on the Champs-Elysées . . .

De Gaulle was not taken in by his own logic: he knew he challenged bodies with words, produced "psychosomatic" effects ("So, Guillebon,[3] we were bluffing. But don't you see, we had to whip up the resigned mass of our countrymen . . . vis-à-vis the Allies . . . kick up a lot of dust"). What is disturbing, nevertheless, are his continual assertion of a worship of greatness, his taste for interpretative systems that fly in the face of realities, the eagerness of his desire for glory. (As an adolescent he already saw himself recognized for having rendered "signal duties": "In short, there was no doubt in my mind that France was to undergo tremendous ordeals, that the important thing in life was, some day, to render her a signal service and that I would have the opportunity to do so"). A great destiny? Yes, absolutely! ("My dear fellow, I am going to tell you something that will surely make you smile," General Chauvin[4] ventured to the young Captain de Gaulle in 1924, "I have this curious feeling that you are fated for a very great destiny . . ." De Gaulle replied, without a smile, "Yes . . . me too.") Me, Me, Me . . . ? Obviously, and that was only the beginning. ("I have understood you . . . *I*, de Gaulle, I open to those people the doors of reconciliation." "Finally, I speak to France. Well, *my* dear and ancient country, here we are together once more, confronting a terrible hardship . . ."). Would that *me* be a God? Such a man saw no drawback to that possibility, Catholic as he was "through history and geography": "I shall extract the *deus* out of the *machina,* in other words . . . I shall enter the stage." And above

all: beware! ("Mr. Foreign Secretary, a State worthy
of the name does not have friends.") Or once more,
when it was suggested to him that he enter the French
Academy: "I am France . . . France does not enter
the Academy . . . Remember Louis XIV." "This is a
matter for psychiatrists!" is Beuve-Méry's diagnostic.[5]
Note the feminine gender of "I am *la France*": *I
am the motherland, I exclude myself from the set of
men.*

And yet, after having woven the net of the mania
where our delusions of grandeur allow themselves to
be caught, he unraveled it. Just like that. His knowledge of history, his experience of pain, his taste for
efficiency became crystallized in a request for love and
a gift of laughter.

There will be no "scapegoat": or rather yes, there
must be one, but it will once more be . . . "myself": *I
shall journey across the desert.*

When "there" is a lack of greatness, when he does
not succeed in imposing his word, this means he is
not loved, and he withdraws. Once, and then a second time, to finish things up: *You shall love me or kill
me, but I shall not be a castrated father. Pétain? No
connection!* Such a thirst for the absolute is appalling,
but on a deeper level it satisfies our narcissistic passions for "all or nothing," our desire for an uncompro-
mising model who runs the risk of getting lost the
better to get hold of us. So much the better, so much

the worse, if it is he who lays himself open to danger
. . . for our sake.

To a people he pulled out of a rout by hoisting it to
the level of his imposing project for France (*France no
longer exists, but I am France, therefore you are great*)
and who calls on them for help in the face of events
in Algeria, he suddenly makes . . . a request. Surprising as it may seem, he puts himself in the position of
a plaintiff. And what is he asking for? He has a
"need," he begs the children to "help" him. "But I
also *need*, yes, I need (he repeats for those who might
have thought they misunderstood) to know what is
going on in your minds and hearts. That is why I am
turning to you, over the heads of all go-betweens.
Actually—as everyone knows—the matter rests between each one of you, each one of you and *myself.*"
(Whew! "Myself" has not been forgotten, even though
it needs "you," on this January 6, 1961.) And again,
"This Algerian régime is given semblance: a small
band of retired generals . . . French men and women,
help me." (23 April, 1961) *Myself, wearing the uniform, was then a man, a woman, like "ourselves," and
he needed help?*

A twofold logical twist, by means of which the person
who is spoken to, flattered at first, finds himself or
herself, thanks to a psychological father, endowed

with a hyperbolic capacity to assist the giant plaintiff into which he or she will turn, provided *help* has been given toward achieving success. No more depression, no more obstruction: *Frenchmen,* a further effort is needed![6]

A major trump card for success: humor. Be it intentional or not, it hands over the word and the flesh of this holder of the highest authority to a seductive divesture, a cunning candor, which reconcile the ardor of a Jesuit rhetorician with bawdy banter, casualness, and grace. Light, perfidious, or black humor: it runs the whole gamut. The man having the greatest sense of humor de Gaulle has known? "Staline, Madame" (to Jacqueline Kennedy). Pompidou? "Protected on top, shored up from below . . . Such as I am and such as he is, I have put Pompidou in office." The supporters of a supranational Europe? "Of course, one can jump up and down on a chair like a young goat and shout, Europe, Europe, Europe."

The conciseness, aptness, and drollness of his speech, a composite of witticisms, rhythmical turns of phrases, and calls for love locate him poles apart from any despotic figure.

Nevertheless, one cannot forever give jouissance to peoples and not satisfy their small daily pleasures: the standard of living, even if it rises, and above all if it rises, is never what it should be; sexual freedoms, the relish of violence, the bliss of untidiness . . . That is not the world of *Le Connétable*. Furthermore, *his* scorn for political parties is only too well known, as are *his* denial of economic planning, his putting the brakes on democracy, his authoritarianism. It thus turns out that the one who claimed he would raise us to the "highest level" kept on bringing us down—using the same devices? Those are among the many ills of "de Gaulle's reign" that more skilful administrators and democratic rulers are doing their best to avoid . . .

"I have succeeded where the paranoid fails." As a consequence, those who are not with me are against reason, *they* talk nonsense, but this is no reason why one should "arrest Voltaire" (or Sartre).[7]

There you have a President who is conceiver and strategist of the national discourse, who creates realities by means of symbols while avoiding the pitfalls of tyranny and modifying circumstances for the good of an increasingly enlarged community, having in mind the interests of its members.

Even if such presidential office, as well as its political conception at the intersection of the nation and the Word, seem cut to the measure of *le Connétable* (which was immeasurable) the deep logic on which they are based extends them and will continue to extend them beyond "Gaullism." One can hope for the emergence of mature peoples who do not need a *someone* to represent or even state the principles of their identity. One can wish that the very idea of nation, saturated through the mingling of economies and cultures, might open up on other unions where the bond between human beings would be located, thus forcing political discourse to move away from national constraints. In the meantime, his understanding of public life compels recognition, it is simply a matter of making it fit circumstances. That is a very difficult task.

Concerning *The Samurai*

An Interview by
Elisabeth Bélorgey

ELISABETH BELORGEY: With *The Samurai*, your first novel, you have forsaken theoretical writing for the sake of fiction. How do you account for that shift from theory to the novel?

JULIA KRISTEVA: While reading Proust's manuscript notebooks I recently noticed the following question in notebook one, leaf twelve: "Should this be turned into a novel, a philosophical essay?" Knowing how to deal with a topic that preoccupies us is an ever-recurring problem, should we treat it theoretically or fictionally? Is there a choice? Is it legitimate to favor one procedure over the other?

Closer to our time, we note that Sartre's *Being and Nothingness* did not prevent *Nausea* from being written; even Merleau-Ponty, who was less or perhaps differently committed than Sartre, considered undertaking a novel, which he never wrote. The imagination could be considered as the deep structure of concepts and their systems. It may be that the crucible of the symbolic is the drive-related basis of the signifier, in other words, sensations, perceptions, and emotions; and to translate them is to leave the realm of ideas for that of fiction: *hence, I have related the passion-filled life of intellectuals.*

Furthermore, I may be forgiven for believing that the French genius consists in a close relationship between common passions on the one hand and the dynamics of intellectual tensions on the other. One finds such closeness nowhere else, even if in certain times, particularly those of national depression—in which I believe we now live—there is, in France, an increasing distance between intellectuals and others. I have thus tried to reconstruct for nonspecialists the work and very existence of intellectuals. Finally, it should be noted that television's ever present, brazen testimony forces literature to walk a tightrope between documents and fabrication, between autobiography and fiction. Nevertheless, as the truth cannot be completely told—at least, that is what psychoanalysis has taught us—a portion of autobiography in a narrative ensures its moorings in reality; but another portion, one of transformation or distortion, that is, the share of fiction, collects the intensity of the subjective bonds that fasten the narrator to others and to himself or herself. And that fictional portion, in contrast with the autobiographical one, acts as a filter that produces a certain discretion, a certain modesty, while changing real-life characters into prototypes.

E. B.: And why have you waited so long, in your work, to shift to fiction?

J. K.: I came to realize, after having completed this book, that I had needed to gain a sufficient distance from myself in order to think of myself as a "character," before becoming an "author." Also, it may be that a certain experience of psychoanalysis has accustomed me to the banality of things, the innocuous wealth of daily chatter, and allowed me to stand back further from the symbolic ascesis that theory consists of. For the time being.

E. B.: According to you, in what fictional category does *The Samurai* belong?

J. K.: I wanted to write *a novel of wide appeal.* Coming from me, that might be considered surprising, especially since it involved a narrative set in intellectual circles. Let me explain: *what I mean by a novel of wide appeal is a sensual and metaphysical narrative.* Appealing in the sense suggested by Victor Hugo: "That huge crowd, eager for the pure sensations of art." Today, the crowds seem to me still more huge and eager, tempted as they are by all the media. Appealing, in the sense that Mallarmé cared about the "necessary anecdote that the reader asks for." Appealing, in the sense that Céline asserted, "In the beginning was emotion."

I wanted, through language, to reach an experience that is infralinguistic and infraconceptual, within emotion, sensation, and perception, one that is, in accordance with avant-garde code, a jouissance often hidden but occasionally admitted. Thus, rereading Mallarmé, I was surprised to find this acknowledgement of his project: "To spin out truly *if possible, through joy,* something lasting for ever and ever, oh! let it happen." Such a state of enthusiasm through immediate access to an undecidable experience, which, on the face of it, is less concerned with formal problems—while being implicitly concerned with them— is a contagion of joy, anguish, and pain; in short, of Eros and Thanatos fused in order to awaken what was traditionally called a "cartharsis" within both reader and writer. In other words, what interested me was to affect the sensory foundation of language while going through a network of memories and fantasies. It so happened that I was teaching a course on Merleau-Ponty's *Phenomenology of Perception* and on the work of Proust, and I had the feeling that I was testing out in practice, by means of *The Samurai,* what I was trying in theoretical fashion to communicate to my students: the connivance between words and sensory rapture.

On the surface, the result is a narrative involving intellectual creation, the conflicts that punctuate the period from 1965 to 1990, the going beyond various theories and preoccupations: structuralism, psychoanalysis, political positions and wanderings, religions, ecology (immersion in the mother-of-pearl reflection of a saltpan, in the beauty of birds on an island . . .), but also feminism, motherhood, an often fiery, obscene intimacy . . . Gradually, as the novel progresses, the theoretical project, the "theses novel," without really disappearing, becomes intimate, internalized, and the story simply becomes subjective, microscopic, and for that very reason, ethical.

E. B.: It becomes incarnate?

J. K.: Particularly in the experience of motherhood—rejected by Carol, chosen as a nearly pantheistic accomplishment by Olga . . .

My attempt to restore the sensory foundation of language made me very attentive to the work of Colette. As for the saga of intellectual maturation, I admire the way Thomas Mann works out his meditation on the body in *The Magic Mountain,* a novel that is little appreciated by French readers who fear German ponderousness: but Mann's Hans Castorp confronts the sick body while the samurai's thoughts were of erotic bodies. Having said that—is it an echo from the avant-garde?—I did not want to build a mountain: rather, I have attempted to construct discontinuities, fragments, fleeting connections, reciprocal reverberations between men, women, space, and discourse, so that the book's emblem would not be a mountain but an *island*. A secret island where characters come together, an island exposed to the four winds, the winds of other chapters as well as the winds of interpretation that readers might insert into the white space, the caesura between sequences.

E. B.: Where do you locate your writing in relation to the "neutral writing" [*écriture blanche*] claimed by Maurice Blanchot and Roland Barthes?

J. K.: Indeed, Barthes's *Writing Degree Zero,* a book that I have much discussed and continue to like, is characteristic of the most demanding literary experience of the post-second-World-War era. In such a "neutral writing," the writer appears as a technician of words, a kind of Orpheus (according to Blanchot) who crosses the Styx into the domain of Hades—the hell of everyday life—and from that journey brings back a few rare trophies that he or she arranges, with many an ellipsis and litotes, in a text made of sparseness and poetry. Such writing is a condensation of impossibilities and, according to Barthes, "follows, step-by-step, the wrenching of the bourgeois conscience"; I should add that it follows, step-by-step, the wrenching of any conscience. Of those partings, it leaves minute, modest marks—precisely quite rarefied. Our silential anguishes latch on to them, during our moments of psychic catastrophes we survive with their indices, in the work of Samuel Beckett, for instance.

One could imagine another trajectory: it is not Orpheus who goes down to Hades but someone who lives in the underworld, such as Pluto, who returns to the surface. I think of Eurydice: instead of again foundering into Hades because Orpheus turned to look at her, if no one cares about her adventure and if, out of loneliness, she comes back up from her painful experience, she need not express herself through a discourse of poetic sparseness. She might well display a fullness of feelings, a surplus of sorrow as well as joy. The solar facet of such an experience is found in Colette, while in the novels of Céline the abundance of horror and abjection is compelling. Finally, in contemporary Russian literature, Varlam Tikhonovich Shamalov, in dry, crude fashion, tells of the Gulag in a language that is technical and drab but full, without ellipses, as in a live commentary, by means of banal anecdotes, and in a saturated vision of evil, which I consider to be more "Plutonian" than "Orphic."

E. B.: Those two types of writing do not imply the same relationship to meaning . . .

J. K.: The facet that I call "Plutonian" appears to me closer to a *writing of contagiousness,* of postmodern availability, which I evoked a moment ago when speaking of the "commonplace." Furthermore, the mingling of Eros and Thanatos that actuates *The Sa-*

murai is of course a consequence of the Freudian understanding of the psyche, with respect to which the claims of a rational power, which might have been an existentialist demand, are untenable. Not one of the characters in *The Samurai* could say "Hell is other people." Hell is within us. No more than one could ask the question, "Should Sade be burned at the stake?": Sade burns within us. Such acknowledgements of cruel truths can lead to a "neutral" writing but also, out of concern for a more immediate—more cathartic—contagiousness and availability, to a writing of fullness and profusion in joy and suffering. Childish, infantile, perhaps it fits in with the permanent childhood within us, with its need for gothic stories and fairy tales: in *The Samurai* Olga writes a book for children that is called "The Samurai."

E. B.: What happens to *the impossible* in your project?

J. K.: It is marked in the composition of the discontinuous, in fragmentation, in polyphony, in the breaks, in the blanks, and in the heterogeneousness that weaves the whole.

E. B.: You write, on pages 214–15:

The advantage of a life (or a story) in the shape of a star—in which things may move without necessarily intersecting and advance without necessarily meeting, and where every day (or chapter) is a different world pretending to forget the one before—is that it corresponds to what seems to be an essential tendency in

the world itself: its tendency to expand, to dilate. The big bang, which has made us as we are and will destroy us in order to write a new chapter, remembering very little of *our* own, is never seen more clearly than in the countless rays spreading outward in a biography full of new departures. The same movement is reflected in a story that keeps making new starts, leaving the reader half disappointed, half eager: he may never find what he's looking for, but as long as progress is being made . . .
Could this excerpt be seen as the image of your book's composition?

J. K.: You are right and, at any rate, that is one of the meanings one can retain from the excerpt.

As far as the *sentence* is concerned, I wanted to remain as close as possible to the spoken rhythm or even that of dreams. On the other hand, I attempted a very particular composition of the *narrative*.

First, I proceeded with brief, swift sequences, I compressed descriptions in order to make them lively and instantaneous. For instance, the first few sentences in the novel, in less than half a page, tell of Olga's leaving her country, her parting from her parents and her lover, her checking her bags, the flight of the Tupolev jet, the three hours of numb boredom, her sole concern being the flavor of the tea, the arrival in a Paris melting under the snow, her discovering that the city of light did not exist, the confusion on the tarmac. All that in a few lines and in one breath. One can imagine, in another narrative, a novelist taking fifteen pages to describe a Christmas evening.

E. B.: Your choice was to compress and diffract at the same time?

J. K.: Yes, the sequences are swift but dense. Like a challenge to zapping and to commercials, which have accustomed us to faster and more fragmented mental operations. I wanted to make of this book an animated, nimble, lively object.

E. B.: With a very unexpected use of parentheses?

J. K.: The parentheses insert and fit in logical remarks or interruptions that were left in abeyance. In dialogues, instead of interpolating clauses such as "he said," "he thinks," "she answered," they just enclose the name of the character who speaks and speed up the rhythm.

E. B.: Is it also done in order to reinstate *your* rhythm?

J. K.: It is rather a rhythm of the times: living our tensions, making use of them. Furthermore, the speed of visual information forces the other means of communication to conform to such cuttings, such sequential montage.

E. B.: An aesthetic benefit?

J. K.: It is a challenge that must be met, and it could also be an aesthetic benefit provided it is supplemented by something that language alone can provide: meditation. Carole's letters and above all the diary of the analyst, Joëlle Cabarus, open up the time needed for reflection, for internalization: in slower motion, more meandering, it is the time during which Joëlle tells about her observations, the sessions with her patient, Carole, or her reading of the Stoics. That thoughtful time is a counterpoint to the fast, sequential time.

E. B.: That diary has a disalienating effect?

J. K.: It is introduced in order to counterbalance the social world, its rhythm as well as its meaning.

E. B.: In other respects, you restore that world abundantly.

J. K.: Through speed and sequentiality I have attempted to compress an important, heterogeneous quantity of information. To open up the files on theoretical debates among intellectuals on certain aspects of society that continue to concern us; in allusive fashion, not didactically . . . To avoid the conventional novel with a linear plot, the disciplined slimness, the clever little melody . . .

E. B.: You not only deal with the instantaneous but also with continuance; the compressing of information recounts nearly twenty years of events and intellectual journeys. But your novel offers another contemporary aspect—polyphonic construction. Could you elaborate on some of these aspects?

J. K.: The real-life characters, easily spotted by critics, are in fact no more than markers along the polyphonic web, which weaves, by crossing and mingling them, three narrative threads concerning three couples that reverberate: Olga and Hervé, Carole and Martin, Joëlle and her set. Olga and Hervé stand for the social side, the one most greedy, most dauntless, aggressive and under attack, a side sometimes ironically treated by the narrator of this intellectual adventure. Martin and Carole herald that segment of our generation that exposed itself most, was most hurt in the sexual as well as political phase of the ordeal: Carole through her depression, Martin by forsaking anthropology for painting, and then for his sexual affairs that lead him to his death; Carole and Martin are at the same time opposites and nocturnal twins, dark doppelgängers of the first couple. Finally, Joëlle and her crowd introduce the reflective aspect of the polyphony: perhaps closest to the narrator, to her caustic, disenchanted tone. There is a certain similarity between the narrator's voice when she speaks of the Montlaurs and Joëlle's tone when she describes the show that surrounds her. Cabarus is a Freudian but also a Stoic who reads Marcus Aurelius and Epictetus; she lives in a world of psychical collapse, depression, and anguish; she is not unaware of the harrying call of suicide, she also knows its Stoic value: it is the moment when knowledge can coincide with the end of the world (if I have understood everything, I have no reason to go on, eternity has been attained); but she rejects the self-confidence provided by understanding, she ventures into care . . . and pleasure. Joëlle is that kind of individual who, with and beyond crises, lives with the greatest lucidity in a state of elation and grace as well as in the suffering such crises offer. She is the element that links the two other couples, she at the same time holds them up and keeps her distance with respect to their pathos, gives them a certain depth and an undefined possibility of coherence. Mikhail Bakhtin would say that there is "dialogism" between those three couples.

E. B.: And the character called Edward Dalloway: is he not also dialogical?

J. K.: His name comes from the surname of Virginia Woolf's famous heroine, _Mrs Dalloway_, but he asserts the typical qualities of a contemporary politician, without for that matter being deaf to women's frailties, at the same time having a beatnik past and being fascinated by Céline's work. Nevertheless, Edward Dalloway is a polyphonic character within himself since he does, in other respects, represent one aspect of the dialogue between the world of the United States and that of Israel, of which our entire generation is particularly mindful and which inserts into the novel the complex but unavoidable question concerning the relationship between contemporariness and Judaism. Ruth Dalloway-Goldenberg is that nomadic figure who has chosen the Law and who fascinates Olga as much as she is seduced by the figure of Dalloway.

E. B.: The United States and Israel, the polyphony of places, Paris, China . . .

J. K.: The French Atlantic coast, the Paris of intellectuals, the childish and pleasant, humdrum Paris of the Luxembourg gardens, all those places change the space of the novel into a kind of kaleidoscope one cannot unify and whose different elements reverberate and contaminate one another.

E. B.: Another ambivalence, constituted of tragic and ironic components, can be perceived all along your narrative thread. Why such tension?

J. K.: The self-irony of characters toward themselves, the narrator's irony toward Olga, Hervé, Bréhal, Scherner, Lauzun, Saïda, and so forth, is a corrosive force but at the same time the most thoughtful form of sympathy and affection. Death, however, checks the light-handedness of such irony. A large number of essential, fascinating characters, who are indeed the real keys of the plot, die during the course of the novel. Meister Eckhart's sermon, read by Sinteuil at the burial of Jean de Montlaur, in which the believer asks God that he "no longer be considered in God's debt"—what a subtle form of atheism in the very heart of mysticism!—introduces seriousness into a narrative that I otherwise intended to be swift, ironic, and aggressive, as my life was and is.

E. B.: Taken in that context, the experience of motherhood reverberates more solemnly?

J. K.: The motherhood theme may be read side by side with the relationship between father and son. The title of *The Samurai* comes essentially from a game that Hervé Sinteuil plays with his son Alex.

Fatherhood as a game: not as a strict law, but as the possibility of playing with the constraint that makes up martial arts and even more so their simulation . . .

E. B. Is there not also another dialogue: between the French tradition (Olga's intentional and success-ful insertion into it) on the one hand, and the Far East on the other, hence the title?

J. K.: Olga explicitly puts in her claim to the French tradition, since she settles in that country. She has an intense liking for the scenery of the Atlantic coast as well as Paris; a playful fondness for her in-laws; simultaneously, that French tradition is overlaid with the images of the East, China, Japan, if only because of the title, *The Samurai*, and that game of martial arts in which, consciously or nonconsciously, the pro-tagonists are engaged. I wanted to suggest that, through the shimmering of those two civilizations, the vitality of a culture can perhaps be measured by the skill with which it interacts with its own memory at the same time as with the memory of other civilizations.

E. B.: How do you reconcile psychoanalysis and literature? Therapy and fiction?

J. K.: The question often comes up as to what psy-choanalysts work with: what is the skill, or the instru-ment, that destines or marks someone out to be an analyst. Obviously, the ability to hear, is what some say; others believe that our erogenous zones enable us to identify with our patients; it is the possible or impossible opening toward our unconscious, is what

yet another group suggests; all of which is probably
true, provided it is brought together; but it can also
be said that one analyzes with one's ability to jeopard-
ize oneself. Freud compromised himself in a fashion
when he excluded himself from psychiatric society
and became interested in sex, which was not considered an object worthy of medical scrutiny; all the
great innovators in psychoanalysis did something
against the establishment, something that was not
supposed to be done; Lacan is well known for his
scandalous, surrealist histrionics, which he introduced
into his analytical practice in spite of the inflexibility
implied in his teaching; D. W. Winnicott, W. Bion,
Melanie Klein were heterodox figures: each one, in
his or her own way, went against the norm, in theory
certainly but especially in their life experience, and
this differentiates them from those who repeat the
doxa . . .

I felt that I could not continue listening to the
novelty and the violence that my patients brought
me—without reducing them to what I already knew
or to what books written before had said—unless I
chanced my own lot. A way of jeopardizing oneself is
to reveal oneself by means of a fiction that shows
facets of that private depth on the basis of which I
understand others, their sorrow, their perverseness,
their desire for death, which are in collusion with
mine. For me, at the time of *The Samurai,* the novel
was a prerequisite for continuing to have a live, in-

ventive listening, one that would be receptive to changes in patients and their symptoms. Thus understood, fiction amounts to a rebirth of the analyst's very personality, a new awakening of her unconscious that ventures beyond sublimation and gives new life to her interpretative capability. Clearly, fiction sets up a new link with the patient: neither lacking in seduction nor, on the contrary, in inhibition, it is a wager on the ability to experience intensely both transference and countertransference. To be revealed in one's greatest self-deprivation is to wager on the greater power of the transference relationship as well as on the possibility of mastering, and therefore increasing, its therapeutic value.

E. B.: Anne Dubreuil was an analyst, but what you say bears little resemblance to *The Mandarins* (in which a character was named Anne Dubreuil), to which you nevertheless refer.

J. K.: There is an allusion to Simone de Beauvoir's *The Mandarins*, but there is also one to Virginia Woolf since Olga's lover is named Dalloway, after the novel *Mrs Dalloway*, and Olga's musing (on Heraclitus' notion of time, or the mourning that, beginning in our childhood, causes us to speak) open up on a fragile, elusive continent . . . I should admit that I feel, intimately, closer to another Simone, the mystical Simone Weil, with her populism, her religious wanderings and errors, rather than to a rationalist such as Beauvoir. Imagining any sort of resemblance with *The*

Mandarins would be, in my view, pretentious and above all illogical; now, for Joëlle Cabarus, a psychoanalyst and a Stoic, a logical error amounts to a moral failing. The fact remains nevertheless that Beauvoir's *The Second Sex* was for me, as for many, an indelible lesson in feminine dignity. Furthermore, the evidence provided by Sartre and Beauvoir to the effect that, in a couple, there can be room for two remains yet and ever a scandal and a problem. That is where relations stop and differences begin.

I do not believe it is possible for a rational system, based on the data of consciousness, to respond to the evil and horror that exist in the world. If hell is within us, the issue is not "to avoid driving auto workers to despair" but to cross the abyss of depression with those who are still able to ask for help, while giving consideration to broad solutions in the social realm, but in more modest fashion since too many hopes can easily lead to delusions. . . . More than equality, the generation of *The Samurai* is interested in sexual differences. Motherhood is not necessarily ordained by fate, it can also be chosen freely and be a source of personal and social blossoming out—for the woman as well as for the couple and the child—no matter what ordeals go with it. Finally, concepts such as the nation, religion, and the family have mustered the existentialists anarchistic aggressiveness; as a consequence, they have cleared the ground for us. Nevertheless, once analyzed and modified, such concepts and such realities can constitute a dam against barbarity.

There is, however, a similarity in the social reverberations of *The Samurai* and *The Mandarins*: it lies in the lukewarm, to say the least, reactions of the media, and this in spite of *The Mandarins'* consecration by the Goncourt literary prize. One can read that Beauvoir is "the Duchess of Beauvoir," "Sartre's muse," "the carpenter ant of existentialism"; her writing is criticized as being "limp," hers is "a botched work," "the dialogues are of a kind heard over and over again in the local pub," there are "appalling errors of syntax," the language "resembles the slang heard in military barracks"; "there is something loose about her style, hands in her pockets, a cigarette dangling from the side of her mouth"; she is a woman doubly frustrated—both by belonging to her sex and belonging to the intellectual establishment . . . and so forth. Certainly the language of the time has changed, but hostility or mistrust live on and are even better organized today. The Mandarins were men and women of power who were fearsome and feared. The Samurai proceed without protection, at the risk of . . . the myth, but also of aggression, paternalism, disavowal . . . Unless it quite simply be what Mallarmé called "the immense human lack of understanding": an age-old, unending phenomenon.

NOTES

What of Tomorrow's Nation

1. [Kristeva's French text reads, "Je ne sais pas qui je suis . . . donc je les suis." *Je suis* means both "I am" and "I follow," so that the final phrase could be interpreted as meaning either "I follow them" or "I am them"—the latter being even more awkward in French than in English—LSR].

2. [Jean-Marie Le Pen's National Front was founded on October, 1972, in anticipation of the 1973 legislative elections. During the first ten years of its existence the impact of the National Front was insignificant; in 1981, Le Pen could not collect the 500 signatures legally necessary to be recognized as a presidential candidate. In 1984, however, the National Front received close to 11% of the vote in the European parliamentary elections; in French municipal elections its percentage has varied between 9% and 12%, rising to 13.9% in March, 1992; as of 1988, there were thirty-three National Front *deputés* in the National Assembly but no senators. Le Pen's support comes from those urban areas with a sizeable number of immigrants, from the so-called

pied-noirs (the Algerian-born Frenchmen who left North Africa after the Algerian war), and from those who blame unemployment on an influx of foreigners. The Front's platform includes a call for the end of immigration; giving job priority to French citizens; the progressive return of immigrants to their native lands; and reinstitution of the death penalty. (Immigrants account for about 7 percent of the French population today, roughly the same proportion as in 1931.)—LSR, with thanks to the French Embassy Press and Information Service.]

[Le Pen was a law student ten years before Harlem Désir was born; S.O.S. *Racisme* was founded a dozen years after the National Front and appeals to a younger generation. It seems to function outside political parties and so far has not presented candidates for any elective office. An analogy might be drawn with our own Civil Rights movement of the late fifties and sixties, although there are major differences such as the religious background and intensity of leaders such as Martin Luther King. Harlem Désir issues from a gentler tradition—LSR].

3. See Hans Kohn, *The Idea of Nationalism* (New York: Macmillan, 1951).

4. See *La Mosaïque France* (Paris: Larousse, 1988).

5. "If we have not hitherto had that conscious feeling of nationality, the ideal abstract of history and tradition, which belongs to older countries compacted by frequent war and united by memories of common danger and common triumph, it has been simply because our national existence has never been in such peril as to force upon us the conviction that it was both the title-deed of our greatness and its only safeguard. But what splendid possibilities has not our trial revealed even to ourselves! What costly stuff whereof to make a nation! Here at last is a state whose life is not narrowly concentered in a despot or a class, but feels itself in every limb; a government which is not a mere application of force from without, but dwells as a vital principle in the will of every citizen." James Russell Lowell (1865), [as quoted in Merle Curti, *The Growth of American Thought*, 3d ed. (New York: Harper & Row, 1964), p. 468, as epigraph to chapter 19, "The Nature of the New Nationalism"—LSR].

6. "It is the free American who needs to be instructed by the benighted races in the uplifting word that America speaks to all the

world. Only from the humble immigrant, it appears to me, can he learn just what America stands for in the family of nations." M. E. Ravage (1917), [as quoted in Merle Curti, *Ibid.*; Curti identifies Ravage as one of a number of "articulate foreigners, such as the Rumanian Jew, M. E. Ravage," who shared that point of view with many "humble," underprivileged immigrants—LSR].

[In the next paragraph, the reference to an "undestructible union" also comes from Curti's book (p. 469) and is a quotation from an 1869 Supreme Court opinion, *Texas v. White*—LSR].

7. See Danièle Lochak, *Etrangers: de quel droit?* (Paris: Presses Universitaires de France, 1985).

8. [So far, little has been published about *S.O.S. Racisme.* One might consult an interview with Harlem Désir by Thierry Leclère, "Le grand frère," in *Télérama*, August 12, 1987; Ronald Koven's *The French Melting Pot*, in *France Magazine*, Fall 1991, pp. 10ff., (published under the aegis of the French Embassy in Washington, D. C.) places the association in a broader context—LSR].

9. Columbia University Press, 1991. [The French title, *Étrangers à nous-mêmes* is more allusive as there is only one word in French to convey the meanings of four in English: foreigner, stranger, outsider, alien—LSR].

10. Aeschylus, *The Suppliants*, lines 198–203 [I have used the translation by Seth G. Bernardete in *The Complete Greek Tragedies* (Chicago: University of Chicago Press, 1959)—LSR].

11. Charles-Louis de Secondat, baron de la Brède et de Montesquieu, *Mes pensées*, in *Œuvres complètes*, Roger Caillois, ed., Bibliothèque de la Pléiade (Paris: Gallimard, 1985), 1:976 [all quotations from Montesquieu translated by LSR].

12. [The topic of Diderot as a precursor of Freud has not been a major concern to French scholars but has been almost a commonplace of their American and British counterparts. Lionel Trilling may have shown the way in his essay, "The Legacy of Sigmund Freud," in *The Kenyon Review*, II (1940), and more recently in the chapter on "The Honest Soul and the Disintegrated Consciousness" in his *Sincerity and Authenticity* (Cambridge: Harvard University Press, 1972). There is also Leo Spitzer's "Freudian" essay, "The Style of Diderot," in *Linguistics and Literary History* (Princeton: Princeton

University Press, 1967), where, curiously enough, Freud's name is never mentioned. Freud's term *Das Unheimliche* has been translated into French as *l'inquiétante étrangeté*, a phrase that matches Kristeva's vocabulary very neatly but is at a linguistic remove from our "uncanny." My own "uncanny strangeness" attempts to bridge the gap between the French and English Freud—LSR].

13. [Following David Wallace Carrithers example in the "Introduction" to his translation of Montesquieu's *The Spirit of the Laws* (Berkeley: University of California Press, 1977) I have maintained the phrase *esprit général* throughout (just as Herder's *Volksgeist* is generally left in German by English-language commentators—see for instance Nathan Gardels's "Two Concepts of Nationalism: An Interview with Isaiah Berlin," *The New York Review of Books,* November 21, 1991, p. 19). The literal rendition, "general spirit," seems inadequate; as Carrithers points out, Montesquieu tried out several other versions of the phrase, one of which corresponds to the English "mental disposition"—and this sounds better in English than in French—LSR].

14. [The French have been calling such a kerchief a *tchador* (for which the English equivalent is "chador"); that is the word used by Kristeva. I understand, however, that from a Muslim standpoint the word is inaccurate. What the young women were wearing would be called "Muslim dress" or "modest dress." After consulting with Jeanette A. Wakin in the department of Middle East Languages and Cultures at Columbia I decided to refer to it as a "Muslim scarf"—LSR].

15. See D. Schnapper, *La France de l'intégration, Sociologie de la nation en 1990* (Paris: Gallimard, 1991).

16. See the Spring 1991 issue of *L'Infini* [in which Kristeva presented a number of critical essays by eastern European intellectuals under the heading, "Something New in the East?"—LSR].

Letter to Harlem Désir

1. [See note 8 to the previous section. The *Forum* refers to a series of meetings sponsored by *SOS Racisme*—LSR].

2. Louis Althusser, *Montesquieu, la politique et l'histoire* (Paris: Presses Universitaires de France, 1959); Robert Aron, "Marx et Montesquieu," in *Dix-huit leçons sur la société industrielle* (Paris: Gallimard, 1962); Georges Benrekassa, *Montesquieu: la liberté et l'histoire* (Paris: Presses Universitaires de France, 1968); Jean Ehrard, *Politique de Montesquieu* (Paris: Presses Universitaires de France, 1965).

3. Montesquieu, *L'Esprit des lois*, in *Œuvres complètes*, 2:558.

4. Montesquieu, *Réflexions sur la monarchie universelle*, in *Œuvres complètes*, II:34.

5. See *L'esprit des lois*, book XIX, chapter 27, [a relatively lengthy one, in which Montesquieu discusses the customs and manners of "a free people." Although England is not mentioned by name the reference is clear—LSR].

6. [French and U.S. legal categories are of course quite different. "Droit privé," as opposed to "droit public," encompasses both common law and civil law as derived from Roman law—LSR].

7. Montesquieu, *L'Esprit des lois*, in *Œuvres complètes*, 2:582.

8. *Ibid.*, 2:274.

9. Montesquieu, *Bibliothèque française*, in *Œuvres complètes*, 1:110.

10. Montesquieu, *Mes Pensées*, in *Œuvres complètes*, 1:981.

11. [Jean-Paul Dollé is a philosopher and journalist whose activities are linked to the *nouveaux philosophes*. In addition to the book mentioned by Kristeva, *L'Odeur de la France* (Paris: Grasset, 1977), he has also published *Le Désir de révolution* (1972), and *Voie d'accès au plaisir* (1974), among others. Julien Dray is a politician, very active on the extreme left wing of the French socialist party. Roland Castro, a former *gauchiste*, is an architect who is much involved in problems of immigration and city planning—LSR].

The Nation and the Word

1. [A major intersection on the edge of the Montparnasse and Latin quarters, it was named after Colonel Denfert-Rochereau who was famous for his defense of the fortified city of Belfort at the close of the Franco-Prussian war in 1870–71; the Saint-Lazare rail station is at the center of the Paris business sector—LSR].

2. [These were nicknames given to de Gaulle, the first in the

army before the second World War because he championed motorized and armored units, the second in London; the title of *Connétable* was given at the end of the twelfth century to the commander-in-chief of the armies and abolished by Louis XIII in 1627 on the advice of Richelieu. "Charles Lockland," on page 69, is an allusion to John Lackland, King of England from 1199 to 1216, who held no continental land at birth —LSR].

3. [General Jacques de Guillebon was General Leclerc's chief of staff in Africa and Indochina. He was commandant of the *École Polytechnique* (1957–59) before returning to active divisional duties as Lieutenant General. One of his four children, Jeanne-Claude, is married to the artist Christo—LSR].

4. [General Chauvin was a graduate of the École Polytechnique who served in the artillery. He participated in all the military campaigns of his day, including the first World War and Morocco, and died in 1939. He is no relation to Nicolas Chauvin, a soldier in Revolutionary and Napoleonic wars, who was made famous by the playwright Eugène Scribe and gave us the word "chauvinism."—LSR].

5. [Hubert Beauve-Méry was editor of *Le Monde* from 1944 to 1969—LSR].

6. [In the Marquis de Sade's *La Philosophie dans le boudoir* (1795) there is an inserted pamphlet that is considered to be a statement of his philosophical, moral, and political ideas. It includes the often quoted exhortation, "Frenchmen! A further effort is needed if you would be republicans!" See Simon de Beauvoir's essay, *The Marquis de Sade* (New York: Grove Press, 1953)—LSR].

7. [Voltaire settled in Ferney, on the Swiss border so he could easily slip into Switzerland in case his writings got him into trouble with the French authorities. As Sartre became more and more provocative, almost as if he were daring the French government to have him arrested, de Gaulle is reported to have said, "One does not arrest Voltaire"—LSR].

INDEX

Aegyptus (mythological king), 17
Aeschylus, 17, 18, 99n10
Algerian crisis, 73
Althusser, Louis, 53
American nationality, 7–11, 89
Ancien Régime, 43
Another Philosophy of History (Herder), 33
Arabs, 14, 36, 45
Arendt, Hannah, 26, 45, 54–55
Aristotle, 20
Aron, Robert, 53, 57
Asian immigrants, 9
Atheism, 90
Augustine of Hippo, St., 22
Augustinianism, 27, 32–33, 53
Autobiography, 78

Bakhtin, Mikhail, 89
Barbarous, 18
Barthes, Roland, 82
Beauvoir, Simone de, 93–95
Beckett, Samuel, 83
Being and Nothingness (Sartre), 78

Bélorgey, Elisabeth, 77–95
Berlin wall, 66
Beurs, 14
Beuve-Méry, Hubert, 72, 102n5
Biography, 84–85
Bion, W., 92
Black Americans, 9
Blanchot, Maurice, 82
Boaz (biblical character), 24
British citizenship, 11–13
British Nationality Act (1945), 11
British Nationality Act (1981), 12
Burke, Edmund, 26, 45, 55

Capitalism, 40
Caritas, 21–23
Carrithers, David Wallace, 100n13
Castro, Roland, 64, 101n11
"Catastroika," 34
Catharsis, 80
Céline, Louis-Ferdinand, 80, 83, 89
Chadors, 100n14